HOUSES NOW

Edition 2006

Author: Carles Broto
Editorial Coordinator: Jacobo Krauel
Graphic designer & production: Dimitris Kottas
Text: contributed by the architects, edited by William George

© Carles Broto i Comerma
Jonqueres, 10, 1-5
08003 Barcelona, Spain
Tel.: +34 93 301 21 99
 Fax: +34-93-301 00 21
E-mail: info@linksbooks.net
www. linksbooks.net

HOUSES NOW

index

introduction

There are trend setters and there are trend followers. Trend setters rewrite the old rules that trend followers then obey. It is the trend setters that we were looking for in putting together this collection. We were looking for new interpretations, fresh viewpoints, innovations. In short, we were looking for designs that are destined to determine the future of architecture. The results of our search are varied.

Since technical know-how is just as important as artistic vision in any project, we have touched upon every aspect in the design and construction processes to give a well-rounded vision.

From conception to completion, we have included information on material and construction processes in order to complement the design ideas of the contributing architects. Finally, since nobody is in a better position to comment on these projects than the designers themselves, we have included the architects' own comments and anecdotes.

Therefore, we trust that we are leaving you in good, expert hands and that this selection of some of the finest, most innovative architectural solutions in the world will serve as an endless source of inspiration. Enjoy!

Aldo Celoria

Travella House

The site for this house, with its 351 square meters of usable surface area, is set on the gentle slope of a low hill in Castel San Pietro. This low residential zone is characterized by the presence of terraced vineyards facing the landscape. The basis for the design was the idea of fluidity, both inside and out, starting with connecting the access road to the vineyards.

All of the infrastructure necessary for living is condensed along a transversal strip. This topography even spans the domestic spaces: the road and parking area, the stairs, the edge of the water, views from the terrace, the living room, the slope of the hill and the border of the vineyard. All the spaces are interconnected, communicating with each other in a dynamic sequence of solids and voids.

The interior spaces flow from narrowness to expansion, always creating different relations within the overall context. The structure and distribution are defined by a continuous concrete wall, which integrates the primary functions and furnishings of the house. Its thickness varies to create a volumetric and plastic interplay in a constant state of flux, from the bookshelves to the stairs, from the fireplace to the kitchen and finally becoming the outermost wall on the terraced roof.

On the second floor, where the bedrooms are, natural light is provided by a constellation of windows that determines very specific views toward the landscape.

The facade is composed of two complementary parts. Continuous glazing wraps around the perimeter of the ground floor, providing very pure and direct views. The upper floor, in contrast, has been fragmented into a cladding of copper pieces that reflect the sunlight in ever-changing shades. Over time, each piece will oxidize differently, creating a vibrant surface that will change with the years.

Location:
Castel San Pietro, Ti, Switzerland
Architect:
Aldo Celoria
Collaborators:
arch. Federica Giovannini
arch. Moreno Lunghi
Engineer:
ing. Paolo De Giorgi
Contractor:
Gianini & Colombo SA
Metal system:
Giugni SA
Sanitary system:
Maroni-Rilav SA
Electrical system:
Sulmoni SA
Facade coating:
Antonio Corti SA
Clients:
Paola e Rocco Travella
Size:
351 m² overall useful surface
Photographs:
Milo Keller

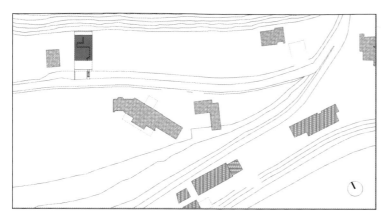

Site plan

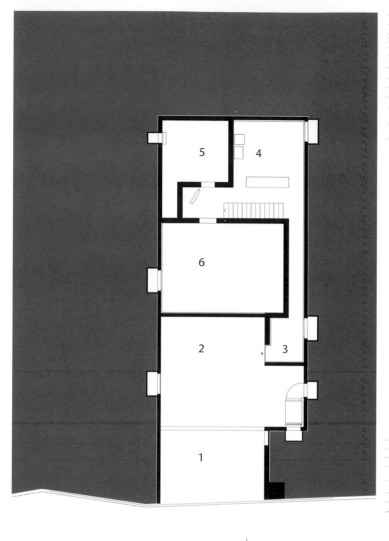

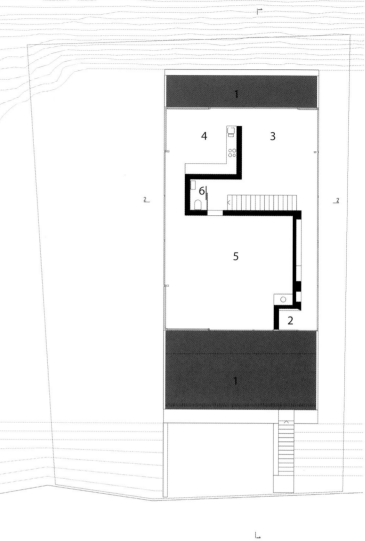

Basement plan

1. Car access
2. Garage
3. Entrance
4. Laundry
5. Atomic shelter
6. Multipurpose room

Ground floor plan

1. Terrace
2. Entrance
3. Dining
4. Kitchen
5. Living
6. Bath

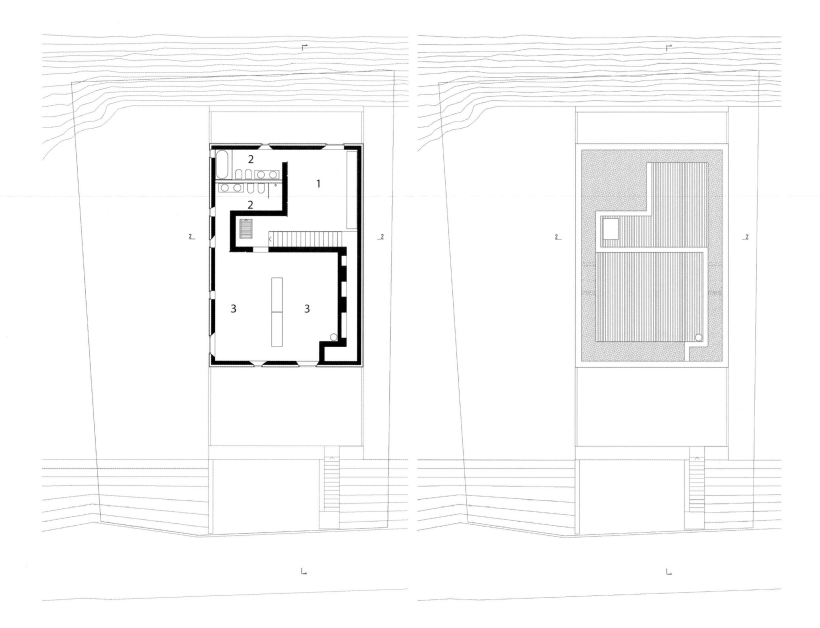

First floor plan

1. Main bedroom
2. Bath
3. Children bedroom

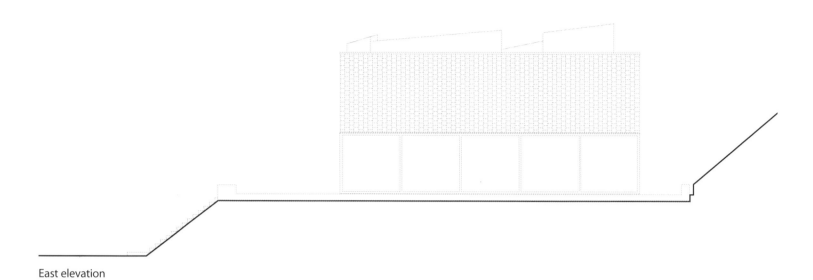

East elevation

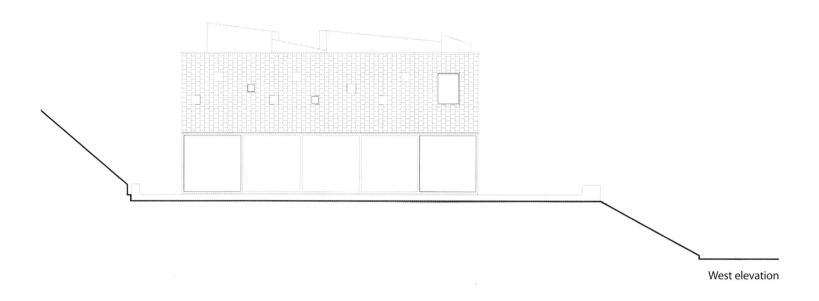

West elevation

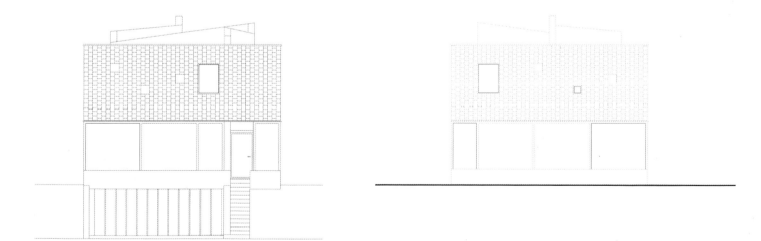

South elevation

North elevation

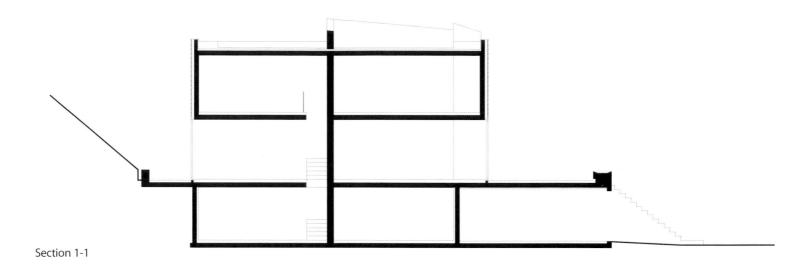

Section 1-1

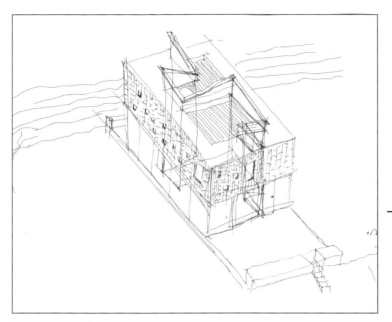

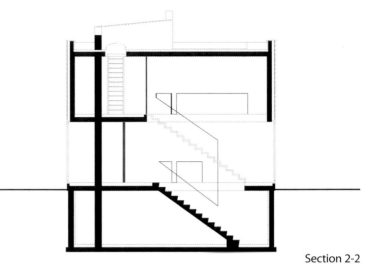

Section 2-2

Takao Shiotsuka Atelier

Blue House

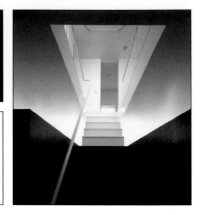

The considerations that most immediately affected the eventual form that this thoroughly modern house in Oita Prefecture would have were the client's demands, combined with the conditions of the site and the function of each space within the house. The final ingredient was the architect's own interpretation, which brought together the variegated requirements into a cube measuring 7.7 m² in plan. Built on two layers, with an additional crowning volume, the constructed area of the house measures 170 m² in total.

Blue, a particular favorite of the client, was chosen for the exterior wall and has been applied in wide strips in a complete range of tones, from greenish blue to blue-purple, with pure basic blue in between. Just as the surroundings and sky are never monochrome, this varied tone-scheme seeks to emulate the natural shifting colors and lighting effects seen throughout the day.

The spatial composition between the floors could not be more different. The ground floor is one continuous space with a non-bearing body placed directly in the center, dividing the zones into their various functions. The living room and kitchen are set on either side on the first floor, while this same box form is inverted on the second floor, becoming an open space growing outward and upward from the ceiling. This central box within the box repeats the relation of the house's cube-like body sitting in the center of its site, with the surrounding space being divided into various outdoor functions and gardened zones.

The second floor is filled with a series of smaller rooms, each visually and functionally distinct, as symbolized by the different color of carpeting in each. The central volume capped by a glazed body floods the second floor with light.

Location:
Saiki-city, Oita Prefecture, Japan

Architect:
Takao Shiotsuka
(Takao Shiotsuka Atelier)

Structural design:
Shigenori Oga

Equipment design:
Yorimichi Kawano

Surface:
170.46 m²

Photographs:
Toshiyuki Yano / Nacása & Partners

1. Parking
2. Front garden
3. Garden 1
4. Garden 2
5. Garden 3
6. Entrance hall
7. Drawing room
8. Living room
9. Dining
10. Kitchen

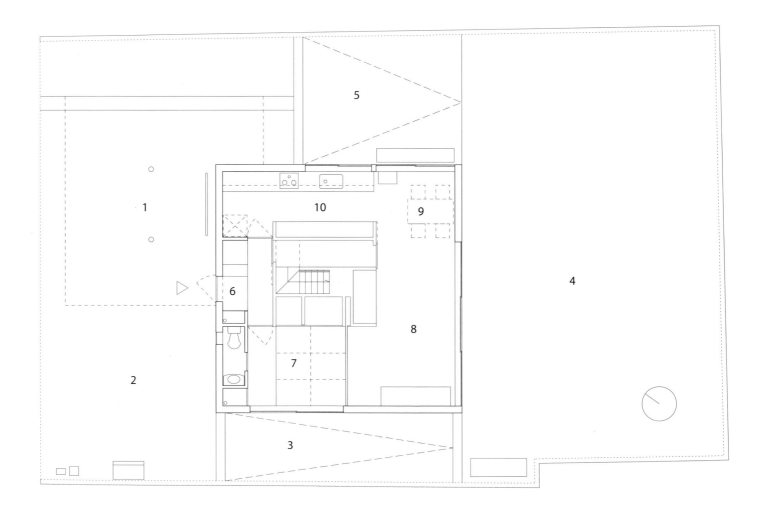

Ground floor plan

11. Bedroom1
12. Bedroom2
13. Closet
14. Study
15. Main bedroom
16. Closet
17. Bathroom
18. Drying space

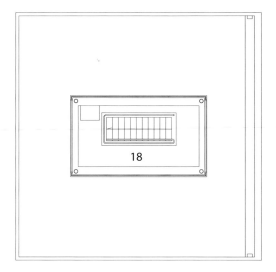

Third floor plan

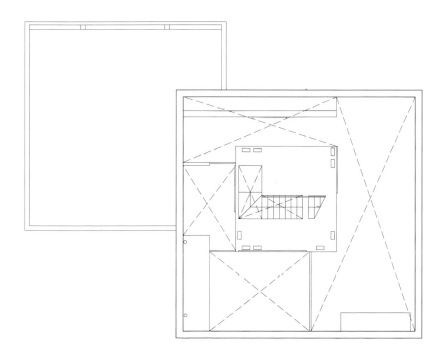

First floor plan

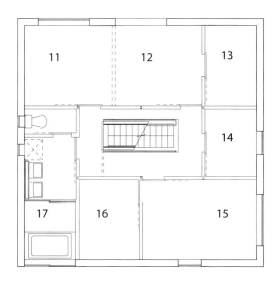

Second floor plan

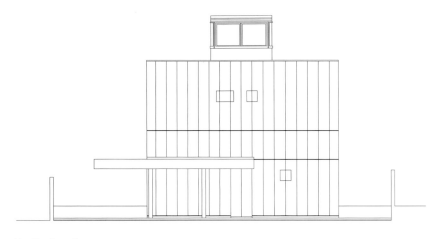

North elevation

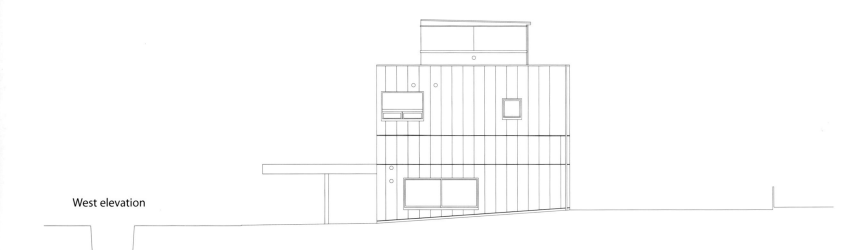

West elevation

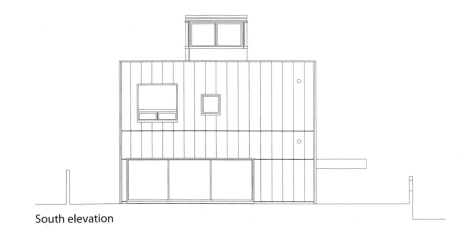

South elevation

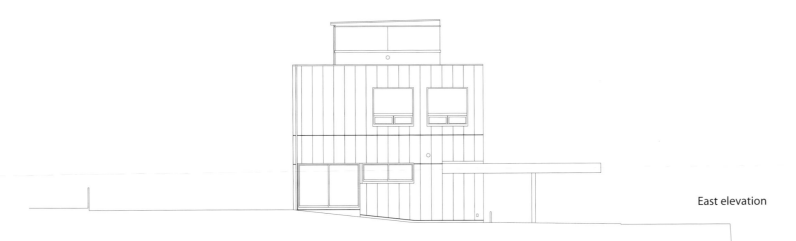

East elevation

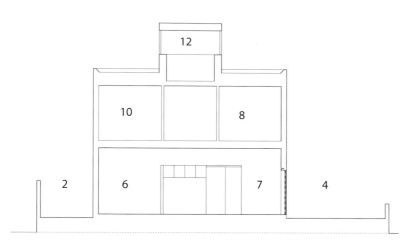

Sections

1. Parking
2. Garden 1
3. Garden 2
4. Garden 3
5. Drawing room
6. Living room
7. Dining
8. Bedroom2
9. Study
10. Main bedroom
11. Bathroom
12. Drying space

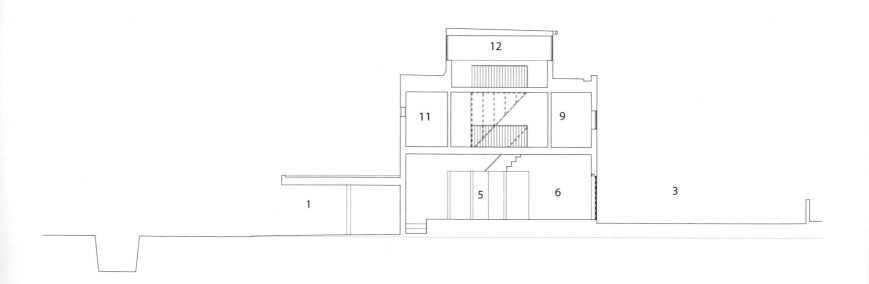

Safdie Rabine Architects

Simon Residence

This single family residence is located on a canyon, perched above the ocean in Scripps Estates of La Jolla. The house steps upward from the street towards the canyon summit and is divided into two parts that are connected by a glass vestibule. The main part of the house curves along the canyon's edge in order for each room to enjoy views of the ocean beyond, while the guest rooms, art studio and garage are located in a rectangular block towards the street. As the house wraps around the site, it creates an internal southern courtyard protected from the ocean winds. The entrance sequence from both the street and the garage are ceremonial, following the slope of the site. A winding stone path climbs through wild grasses and cactuses to the front door and squeezes between two walls, the wood wall of the front house and the curved plaster garden wall. From the garage, a gently stepping wood and stone gallery also leads to the entrance vestibule. The entrance vestibule acts like an elbow linking the different areas of the house, both inside and outside, offering the first glimpse of the canyon and the interior courtyard on arrival. Stone floors and wood walls extend inside and outside and define circulation throughout the house. The ceiling in the main house curves upwards towards the canyon, emphasizing the views of the ocean, while a low ceiling along the circulation provides space for clerestories and a more intimate scale for the house. The single story structure hugs the landscape, allowing the dramatic canyon and ocean views to take center stage.

Location: Scripps Estates, La Jolla, California, USA
Architect: Safdie Rabines Architects
General Contractor: Wardell Builders, Inc.
Interior Design: MPLA
Landscape Designer: Aerea
Biologist: Dossey & Associates
Archaeologist: Affinis
Appliances: Standards of Excellence
Door Hardware: Bellisima
Cabinetry: Wood Design West
Ceramic Tile: Wichert Tile
Cork Flooring: Floor Tech
Decorative Concrete: Concepts in Concrete
Garage Door: ADS
Interior Doors: Saroyan Lumber
Plumbing Fixtures: JC Plumbing
Sliding/Fence/Deck: J & W Redwood
Stone Paving: Rens Masonry
Windows/Ext. Doors: A & A Glass
Photographs: Undine Pröhl

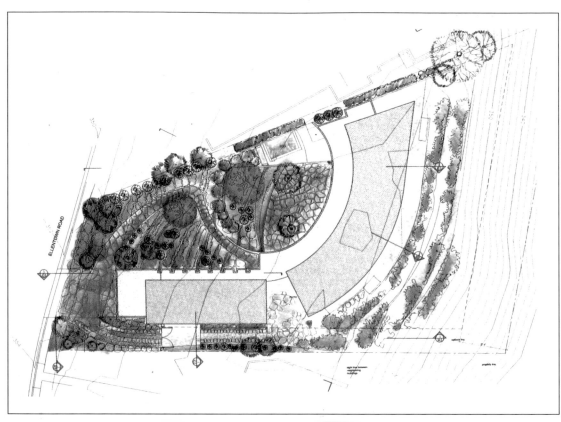

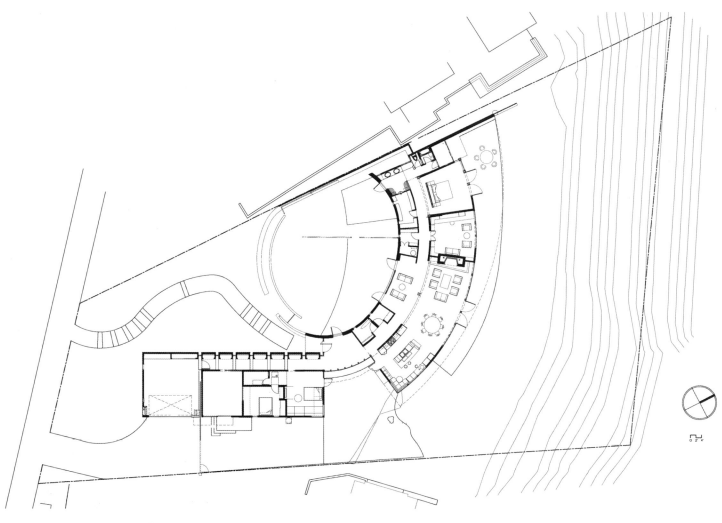

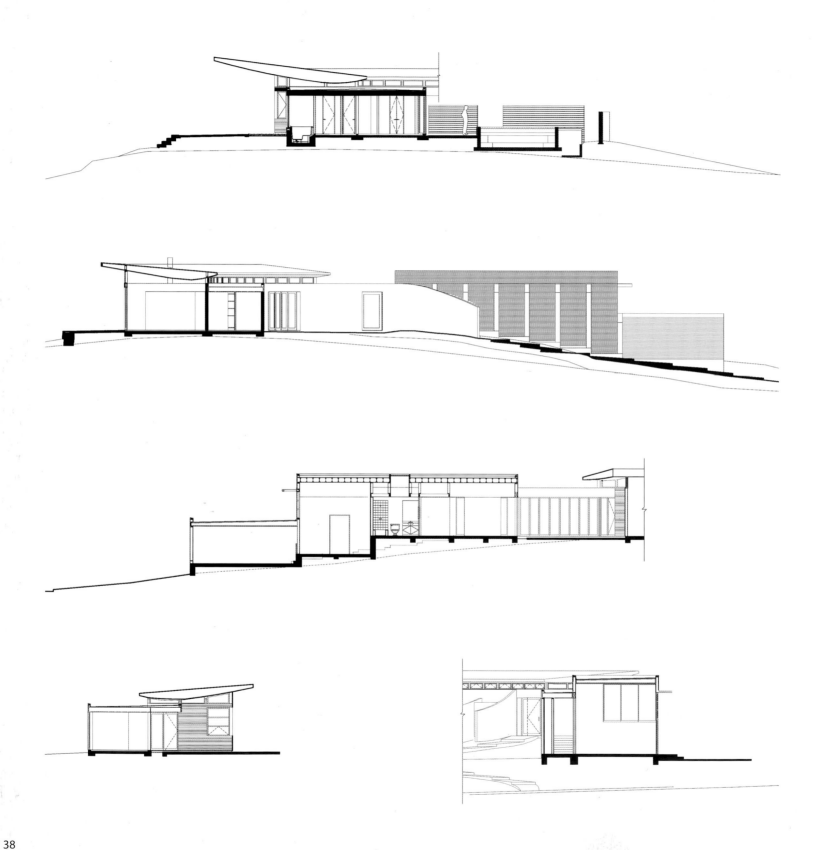

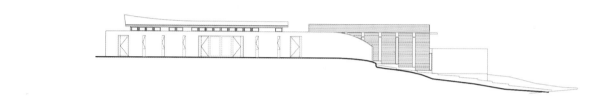

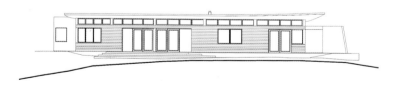

Roberto Tognon Architetto

Ruzza House

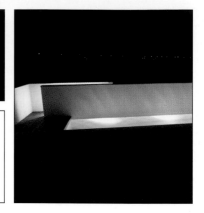

The program for this house located in the city of Padua is based on the links dictated by the particularities of the zone's ground plan, which determined the placement and orientation of the site.

The volume is delimited by four retaining walls and enjoys full autonomy in relation to its surroundings. A white rectangular body is set on the north side just a few meters away from the wall, yet linked to it via a glass roof. The architect designed an interior composed of a box arranged on three independent levels, interconnected by an enclosed stairwell as nucleus: the underground level, lit by a transparent ceiling, is occupied by installations and services; the central level contains the living room, dining room and kitchen, and the uppermost floor houses two bedrooms, each with their own bathroom, and a spacious suite with a walk-in closet and ample bathroom. Each floor features a repetition of the layout defined by the line of interior pillars that divide the floor plan into two sections: a wide strip and another narrower space distributing the spaces and functions in a clear and orderly way, following the lengthwise orientation of the floor plan.

The primary characteristics of this building are permeability of space and the possibility of passing through it at various junctions. To achieve an effective feeling of continuity between interior and exterior, a homogenous use of colors and materials was decided upon, with white predominating. In effect, white was used in all elements, including the travertine marble paving, thereby helping to define the composition by its clarity and unity. The flooring finds its continuity on the exterior – specifically, in a large courtyard enclosed by white walls, with a small gardened space culminating in a swimming pool opposite the house. This area is well lit by night, creating a relaxing and pleasant vista that can be enjoyed from inside the house.

Location:
Mandria, Padova, Italy
Architect:
Roberto Tognon Architetto
Collaborators:
Ing. Strutturale Marco Franceschini
Construction:
2004
Surface:
400 m²
Photographs:
Claudio Mainardi

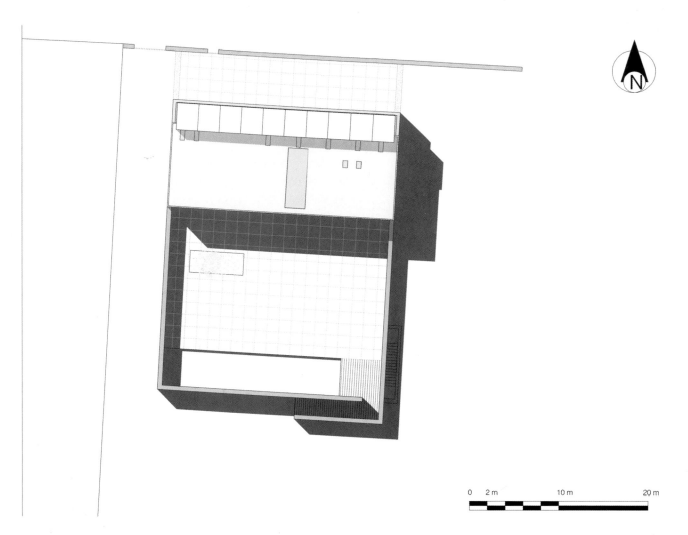

0 2 m   10 m   20 m

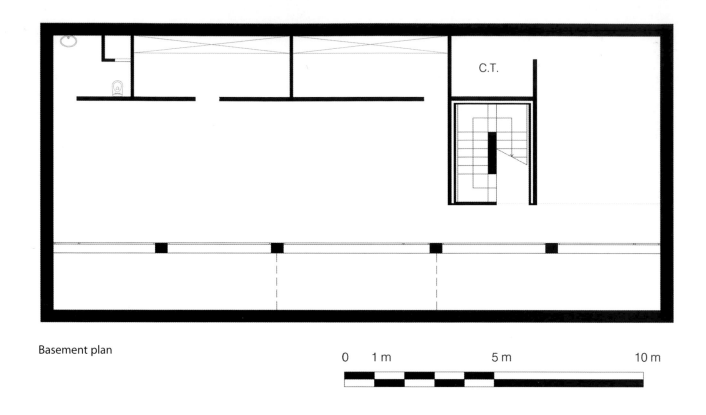

Basement plan

```
0    1 m              5 m                    10 m
```

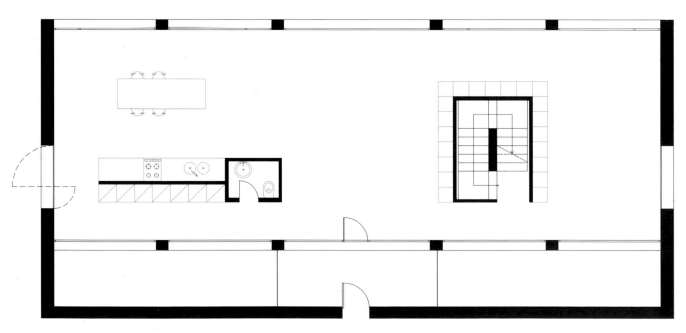

Ground floor plan

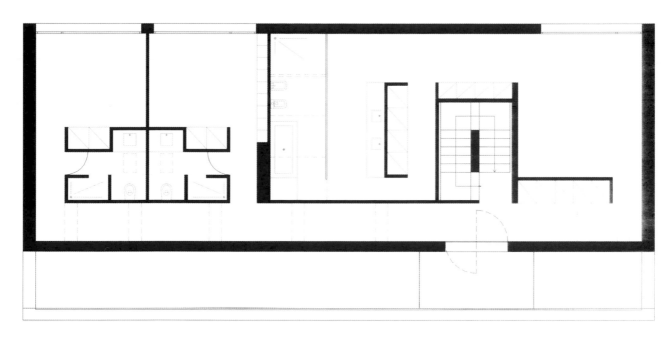

First floor plan

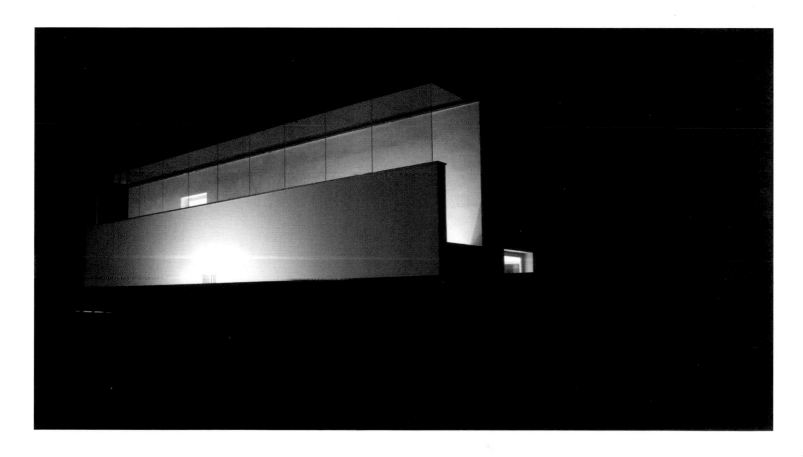

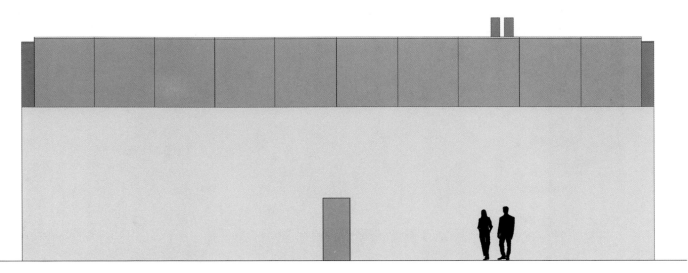

North elevation

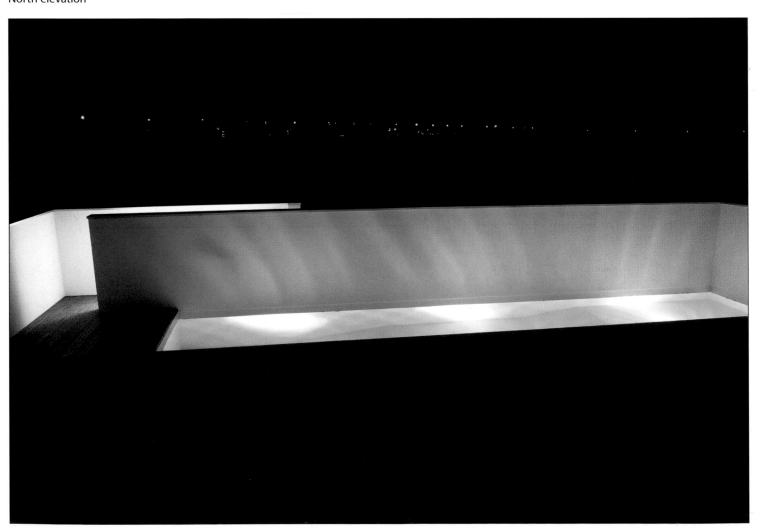

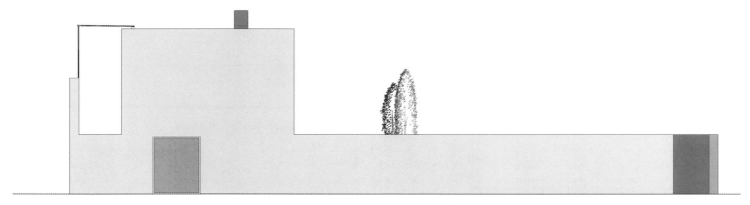

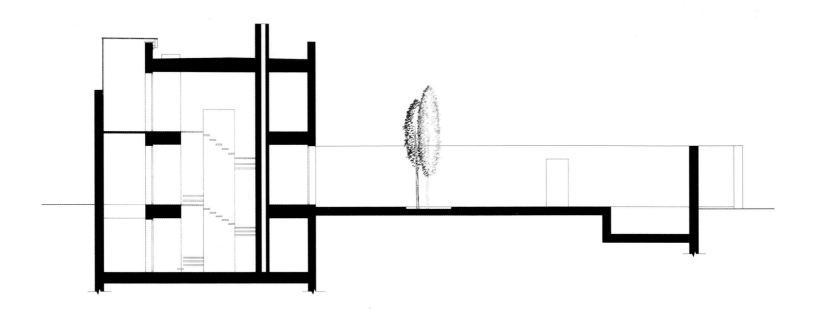

Bottega + Ehrhardt Architekten

House M

House M combines the old and the new and places itself as an independent new house.

Situated half way up the hills of Stuttgart, House M has a view over the entire urban center.

It is a brick building of the late fifties with a new roof extension. The two main levels were cleaned and redistributed. The roof was taken off and replaced by a square box of steel and glass.

An aluminum box only open on one side contains the owner's office and gives the building a new identity. The new roof advances over the western side and uses this gesture to point out the new entrance door.

A massive black steel stairway, not connected to the ground, leads into the office-loft, a cream white and horizontal space with a glazed facade, with an overwhelming view over Stuttgart and the Neckar river valley. The glossy epoxy floor adds to this lightflooded space.

A bare construction made of steel angle irons and corrugated iron acoustic panels subdivide the room into working areas.

Entering the main apartment, a direct view through the entire house shows its depth.

Another stairway made of steel with smoked oak steps connects the two levels and ends in a concrete pedestal - an observation platform in the children's playroom.

The stairway is accentuated by a lightbox showing the old house before its face-lift.

Generously glazing on both sides opens the city view to the north and the garden to the south. All components are made of white varnished density fiberboard, a good contrast to the industrial smoked-oak parquet.

A sliding door of mirror glass separates the master bedroom from the hall. The bedroom is defined by a central volume, usable from both sides, containing bed, dressing room and washstand, with integrated sliding doors that divide the room into three areas. The chestnut veneer surfaces of the wooden furniture contrast with the gray concrete floor.

Downstairs, at the lower garden level, next to the children's room, there is a small au pair apartment and the rooms for the functional systems.

Grates made of bankirai wood connect all the levels to the outside. The clear glass balustrade around the terrace leaves the view unrestricted.

Location:
Stuttgart, Baden-Wuerttemberg, Germany

Architects:
Bottega + Ehrhardt Architekten
Giorgio Bottega, Henning Ehrhardt

Project Architect:
Christoph Seebald

Construction Supervisor:
Jo Carle Architekten

Structural Engeneer:
ZP, Zindel & Partner

Design: 05.2002

Construction: 04.2003 - 05.2004

Size:
Main house 245 m²
Au pair 25 m²
Office 160 m²

Cubic Capacity:
1850 m³

Photographs:
David Franck Photographie

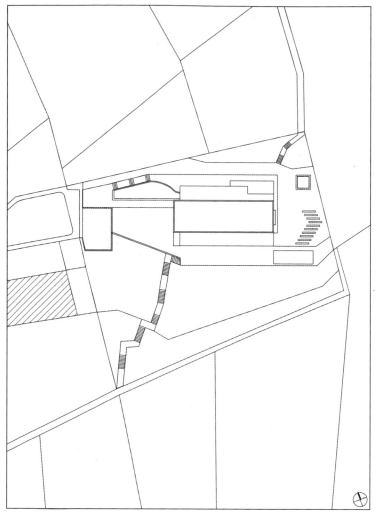

Site plan

On the right a photograph of the house before the renovation

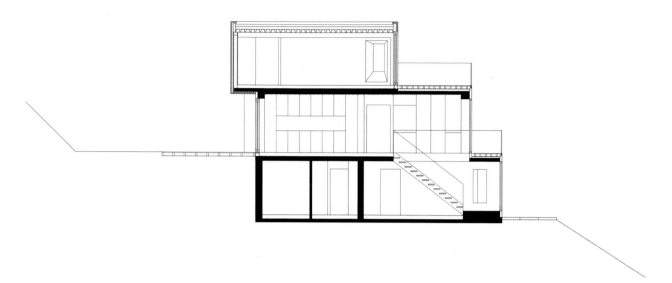

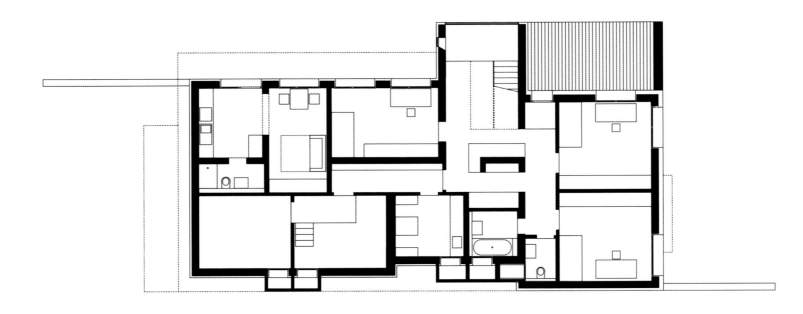

First floor plan

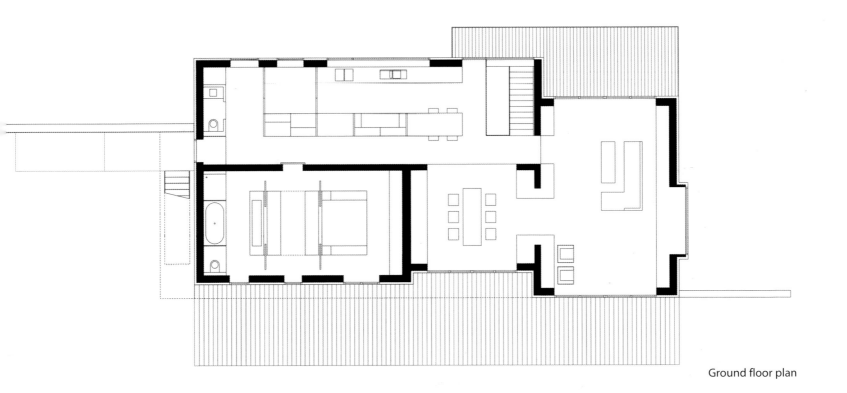

Ground floor plan

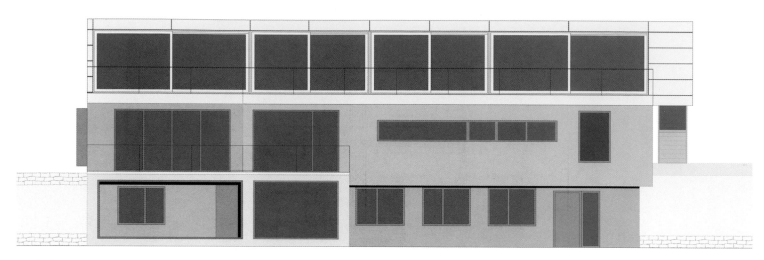

North elevation

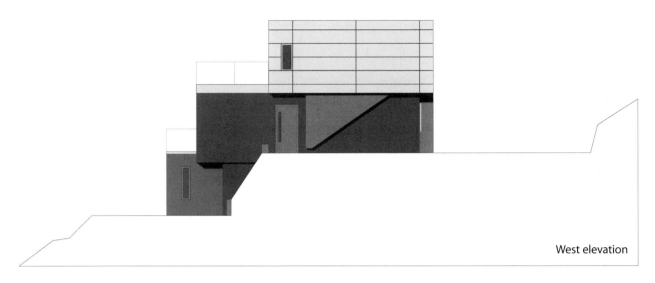

West elevation

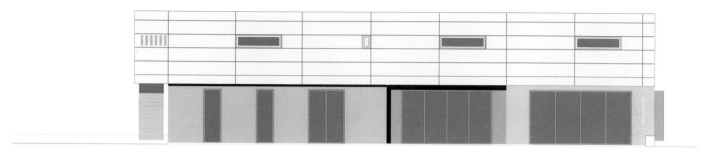

South elevation

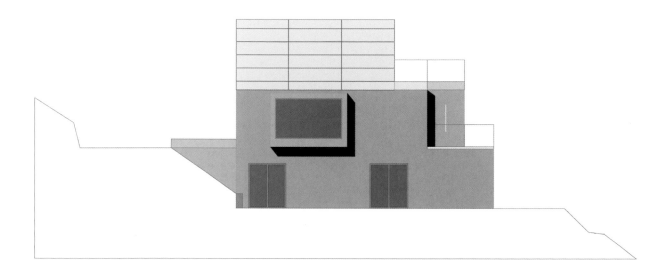

East elevation

Jiménez Brasa Arquitectos

House in Granada

With an ambitious program and a small plot measuring only 4994 square feet (464 sq m), the building had to resolve the conflict between the need for privacy as well as a degree of isolation from El Camino de los Neveros, the road providing access in the northeast direction. The views face the horizon, encompassing everything from the Sierra Nevada to the Alhambra, with a plain and the city of Granada in the opposite direction.

Laid out like strips running parallel to the street, the spaces filter out noise and soften the visual impact of a building that presents, in the foreground, a plane of glass as separation from the street and a long, narrow garden. This is the most hermetic face of the building, the one housing the service areas and entryway; from here, the house is interpreted as an intermediary that administers a privileged relationship with the landscape.

The various pieces laid out on this floor – living/dining room, kitchen, the daughters' bedrooms, guest rooms – are all set on a double platform that conforms to the slope of the terrain and stretches outward to the lower edge of the plot. Pergolas protect the practicable wall sections of the living room in a plane raised 13 feet (four meters) from the lower street, from which the garage is accessed.

The vestibule, which gives order to and connects the spaces of the entire house, includes a lightweight stairwell leading to the master bedroom and continuing upward to the roof terrace, which is clad in a floating wood flooring and features a swimming pool. This entire volume is perched above the bedrooms of the lower floor.

With heights of up to eleven and a half feet (3.5 m), the spaces in the semi-basement complete the program with a gym, study and garage. They receive natural light and ventilation via courtyards that have been opened up along the side garden like planes of passable glass that serve as light boxes for the small gardened spaces of the plot.

Location:
Granada, Spain

Architects:
Jiménez Brasa Arquitectos
Yolanda Brasa Seco
Eduardo Jiménez Artacho

Promoter:
Emilio González / Belén Martín

Construction completition:
2003

Constructor:
Fernandez Adarve SL

Photographs:
Fernando Alda

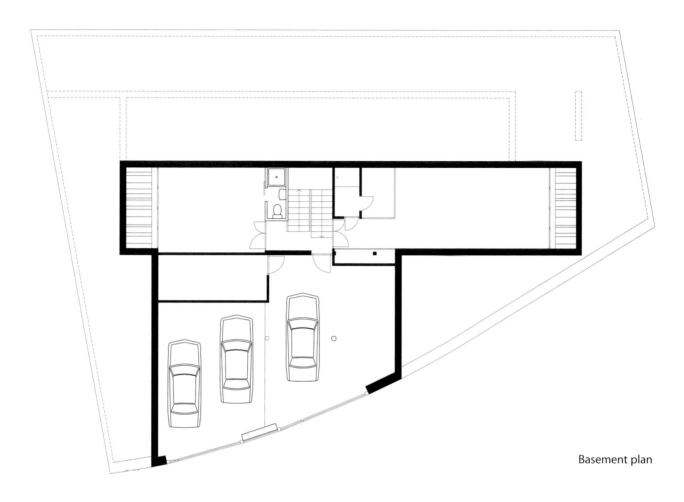

Basement plan

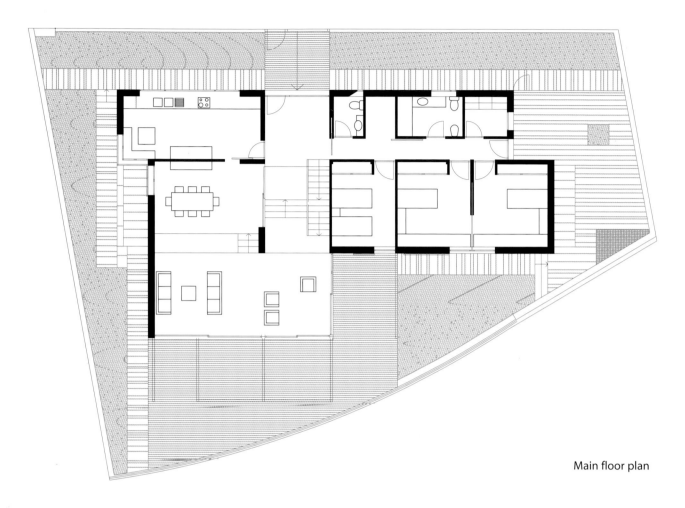

Main floor plan

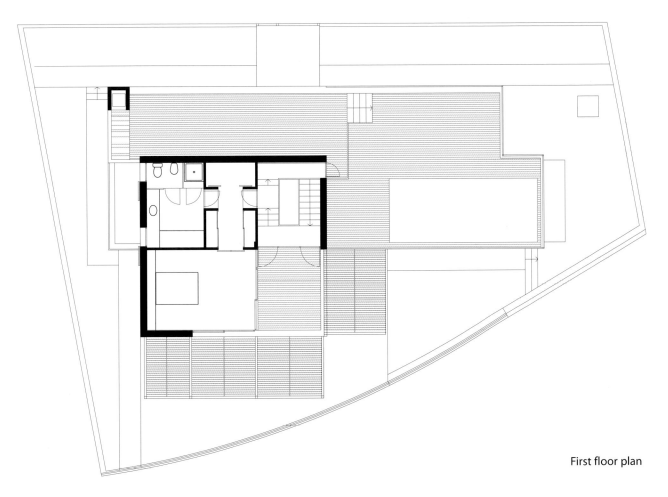

First floor plan

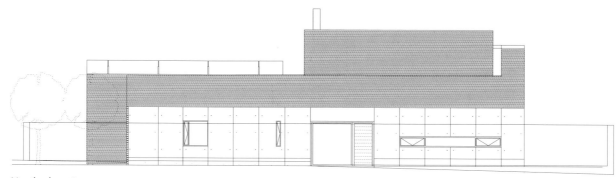

North elevation

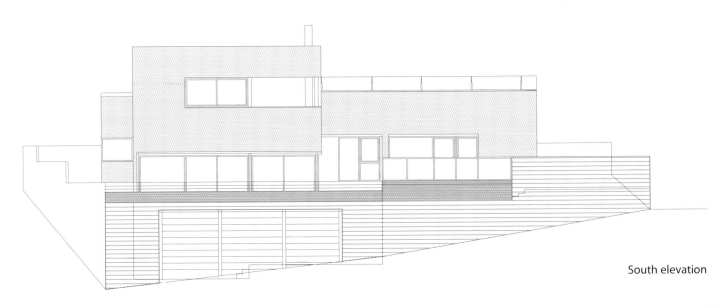

South elevation

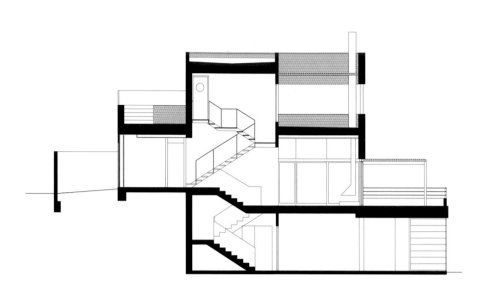

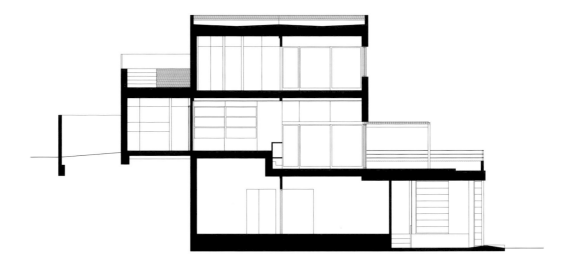

David Soldevila

House with studio in Tiana

The house is located at 260 m above sea level, on the southern slope of the Marina mountain chain. On the border between the Barcelonès and Maresme areas, its position enjoys a privileged view over the whole bay of Barcelona, from the Montjuïc mountain to the village of El Masnou

The 2200 sqm lot above the Mas Ram housing estate is entered from the back. The gentle slope on two thirds of the site is protected woodland and unbuildable; the house occupies the remaining 23-meter cliff; well sheltered from the north and northeast winds, it faces the southern and southeastern views. The construction's two wings form a V shape under a single roof, creating a sheltered outdoor space.

The two rectangular units, 14 x 4,20 x 5 meters (length, width and height) have minimum northerly openings, to permit some light and ventilation. The southern and southeastern façades are wide open to the view. The two units are intended to have multiple uses, a flexibility achieved by reducing the number of fixed items. One of them is the technical wall that contains the centralized installations (water, gas, and waste). The kitchen is on one side; on the other, the bathroom is further enclosed by the staircase. The indoor distribution finally depends on the furniture and sliding elements.

The completely dry construction system, used in factory buildings, consists of angle irons assembled with nuts and bolts, like a "Meccano". The façades' two skins are of big prefabricated elements. The outside skin consists of steel sandwich panels and aluminum carpentry. After the air chamber that contains the vertical structure, the interior skin uses large wooden prefabricated panels. Based on the "Ikea D.I.Y" idea, the interior's components are easily interchangeable by the inhabitants. The "never finished" building is only a stage in the changing interior life of the house. The dry and un-traumatic construction system allows every space in the house to adapt to the necessities that each new moment requires.

The building's very low thermal inertia means it can be warmed or cooled very rapidly by natural means. In summer, it is cooled by cross ventilation. In winter, the house accumulates solar heat through the big south windows. A stove solves extra needs on cold nights or cloudy days.

Location:
Tiana, Barcelona, Spain
Architect:
David Soldevila Riera
Structure:
Roberto Aparicio Arqtoe.
Construction supervisor:
Josep Mª Pedra
Construction:
Construcciones Universal 85 (foundations), Jansa Metal (structure), Muntatges Montornés (walls), Carpinteries Canyelles (carpentry), TeznoCuber, Fustes Alberch (wood), Instal·lacions Verano s.l. (instalations), D.y X. Soldevila, L. Torralbo, y L. Valbuen (self-construction)
Promoter:
D.y X. Soldevila, L. Torralbo, y L. Valbuena
Year:
2001-2002
Pkotographs:
Stella Rotger

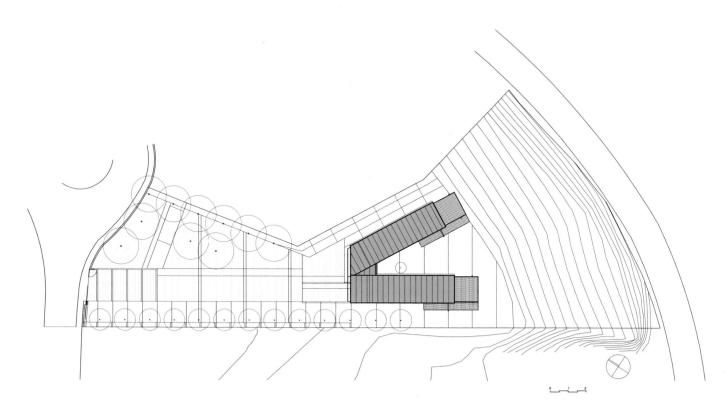

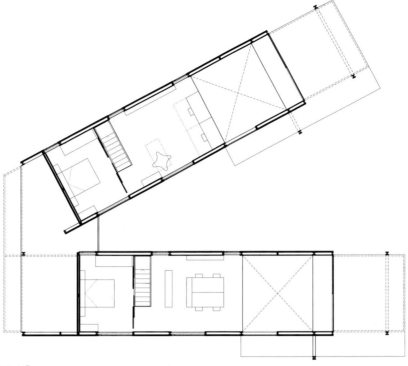

First floor

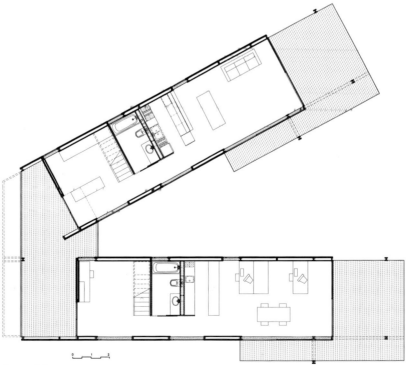

Ground floor

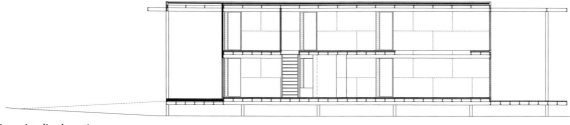

Longitudinal section

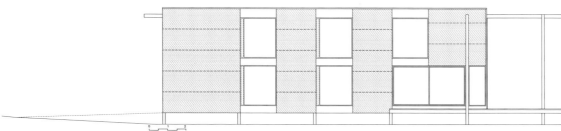

South-west elevation

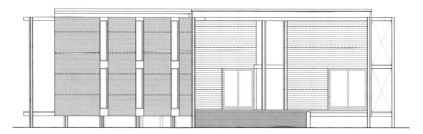

North-west elevation

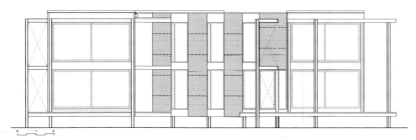

South-east elevation

North elevation

North-east section-elevation

Taku Sakaushi /O.F.D.A.

YAMA

As the site is raised a few meters in respect to the surroundings and the level of the road, privacy is automatically ensured on the ground floor of this light-filled and thoroughly modern home. Thus, at each corner of the site are placed large windows facing ample outdoor gardened spaces.

The second and third floors, on the other hand, are ensconced within pristine white volumes to shield them from views from the outside. An abundance of natural light is brought into these spaces through the incorporation of a vertical light shaft extending through three floors. The spatial dynamics brought about by this ground-floor horizontal openness paired with the sizeable vertical void create the central design theme, around which the house unfolds.

In fact the underlying and unavoidable question of shape and line when drawing up the floor plan was a central preoccupation in the design process of this house. This root question gave rise to the name: Yama, which means 'mountain' in Japanese. Rather than defining the shape of the house, it was meant as a symbolic anchoring concept.

Location:
Shibuya, Tokyo, Japan
Architects:
Taku Sakaushi /O.F.D.A.
Main Structure:
Steel Frame (Partially RC)
Structural engineer:
Nagasaka Architectural Atelier
Constructor:
Kawaz construction
Design:
March 2003 - May 2004
Construction:
June 2004 - June 2005
Site area:
189.63 m²
Building area:
126.88 m²
Total floor area:
217.34 m²
Photographs:
Hiroshi Ueda

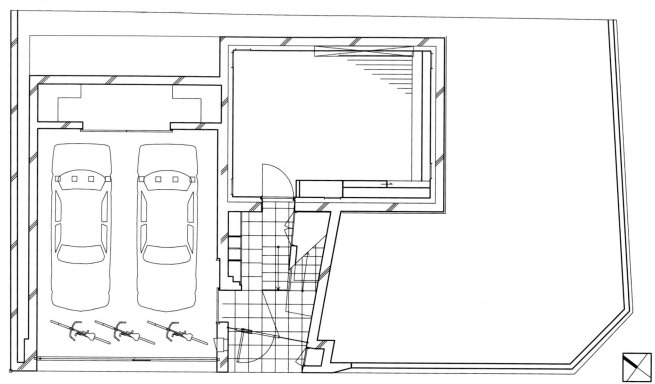

Basement Plan

Ground Floor Plan

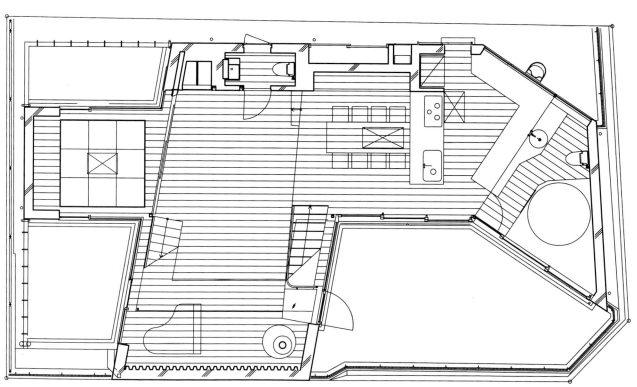

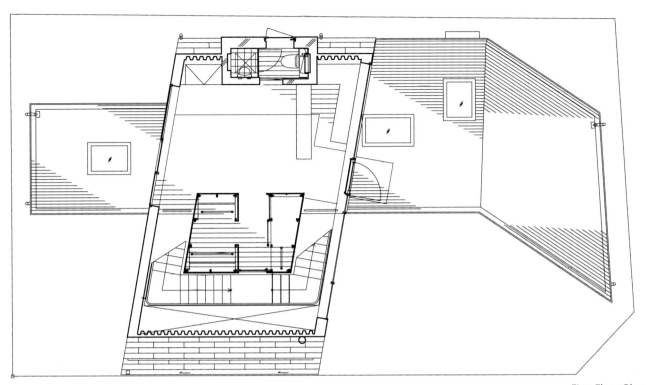

First Floor Plan

Second Floor Plan

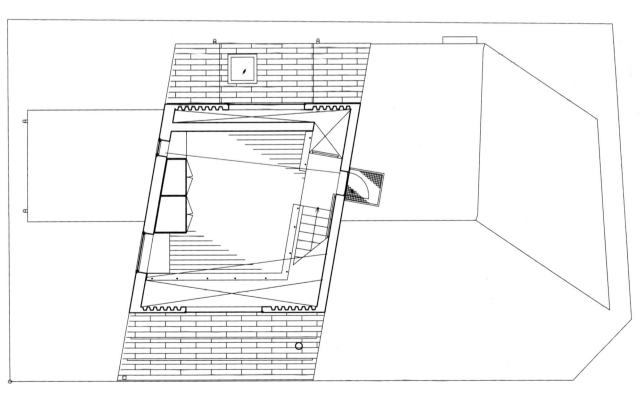

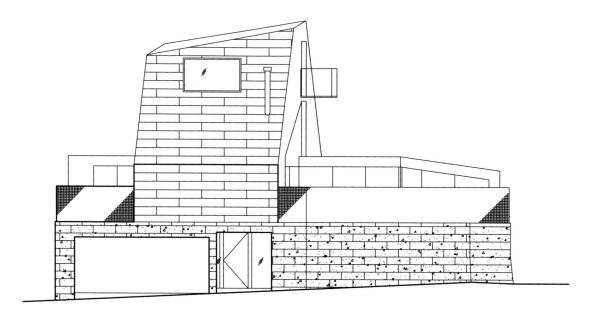

West Elevation

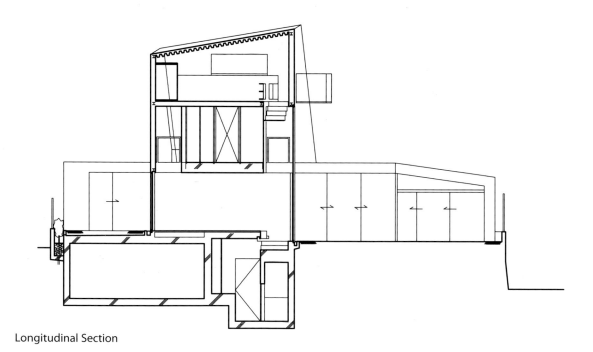

Longitudinal Section

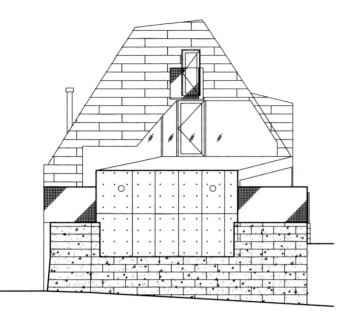

South Elevation

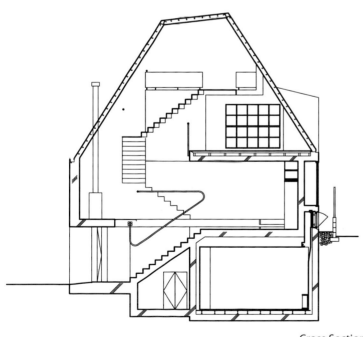

Cross Section

97

ARTEC Architekten

Balic-Benzing House

The southern part of the Burgenland district is a gently undulating landscape of rolling hills and vales, with wide stretches of open countryside between the towns and villages.

The piece of land chosen by a Viennese couple for the construction of their unpretentious holiday home, was located at a short distance from a quiet country road along the ridge of a piece of high ground. The wonderful view extends in a southwesterly direction, descending along the hillsides to dissolve in the distance, far within the Steiermark region.

The distribution of the space is straightforward:

A large room for the proprietors (646 sqft) and a bedroom half that size for their guests. There is an intermediate space in between, which can be opened or closed off by means of sliding doors. The two main units are equipped with bathrooms.

Self-controlled generosity is the quality that defines the terrace. The same uninterrupted plane surface (95 x 26 ft.) is repeated twice, to create the floor and the roof of the indoor spaces and the terrace that circumvents the whole building. The terrace offers a sheltered outdoor space that hovers freely above the sloping fields. The extremely wide overhang of the roof defends the house from excessive solar radiation and overheating.

The connection between the prefabricated construction of the terrace and the underlying terrain is a small storage space made of freshly mixed concrete cast in situ and free standing supports of steel.

The rooms are glazed on the side facing the view, towards the southwest. The side facing the road is perforated by several openings, at heights best suited to particular expected uses.

The terrace railing is a plank hovering in mid-air, which also provides a shelf or a table for people enjoying the terrace. The building seems to float weightlessly above the ground. The horizontality that orients all the main and secondary forms reveals the slopes of the surrounding land.

Location:
Bocksdorf bei Güssing, Burgenland, Austria
Client:
Dr. Renate Balic-Benzing and Emin Balic-Tahir, Vienna
Architects:
ARTEC Architekten, Bettina Götz, Richard Manahl
Collaboration:
Ronald Mikolics, Julia Beer (Model)
Structural analysis:
Peter Bauer
Start of planning: July 2004
Completion: Autumn 2005
Surface area: 14,435 m²
Building area: 223 m²
Converted space: 420 m³
Gross floor area: 127 m²
Floor area: 86 + 14 m²
Photographs:
ARTEC Architekten

First floor

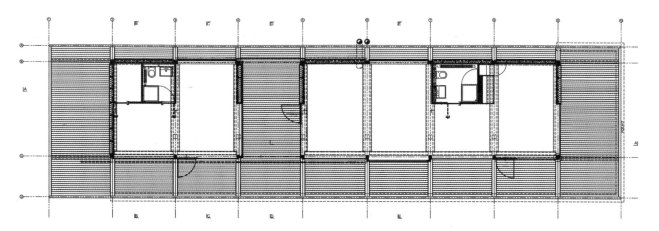

Ground floor

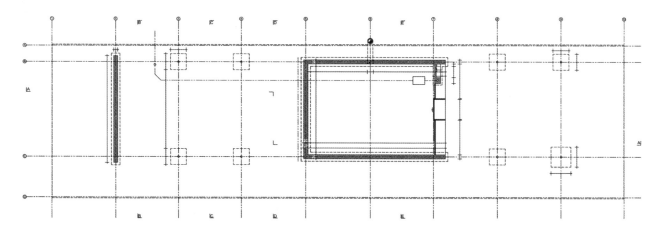

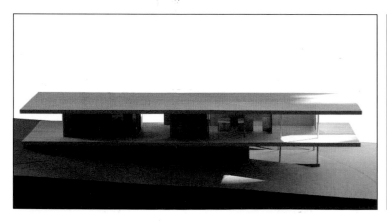

South elevation

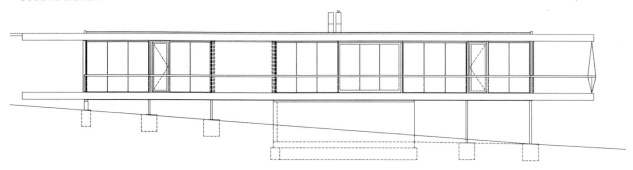

North elevation

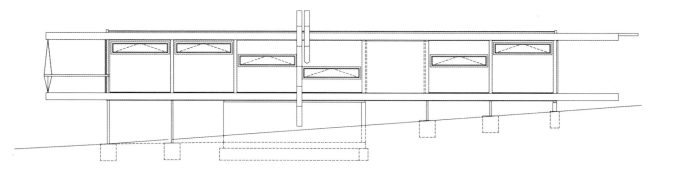

East elevation

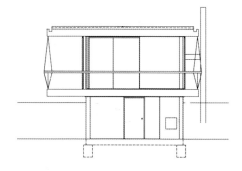

West elevation

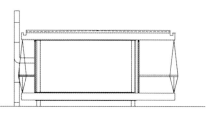

Longitudinal section

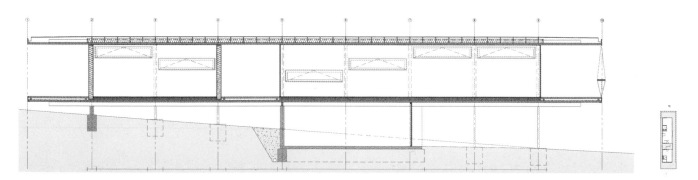

Felipe Assadi
Christophe Rousselle

Serrano House

Built on a 10,760 sq ft plot, the Serrano House is situated on one of the ridges along the eastern side of the city of Santiago. The basic premise of the project is the spectacular 180º view, overlooking the city from a great height. Nevertheless, the probable future presence of neighboring constructions decided the creation of a pavilion with apparently opaque sides, relating to the surrounding context along a single frontal axis.

The operations started by terracing the landscape, to drop the foreground down by one level. The floor level of the house is thus half underground, enclosed visually by the ground it cuts into. At this level, the common rooms are in a mostly transparent space, consisting of steel pillars and glass windows.

The second floor starts from the upper level of the plot, and runs horizontally across the slope, seeming to float above the ridge. This volume is built of reinforced concrete, completely clad with an outer wooden shell. Behind this surface are all the openings, for light, view or ventilation. The wooden shell creates a sort of Venetian blind, which shelters the intimacy of the interior and regulates the entrance of light. On the northern wall, the shell is on runners and can move horizontally across the façade. This level contains the bedrooms, some living spaces and an interior patio for the bedrooms that do not have the city view.

The third level is developed like a wooden deck over the roof of the bedrooms; with the entire western panorama below, this lookout point establishes a more direct relation to the environment.

An upright concrete body connects these horizontal strata. Situated at the highest part of the site, this tower contains the vertical traffic within the house and organizes the relation between the various spaces. On each level of this volume, there is a small living area for the use of the adjacent rooms. On the third floor, there is a studio with direct access onto the roof.

The materials used are reinforced concrete (unrendered), steel, glass and almond-tree wood. The building occupies a surface area of under 10,000 sq ft.

Location:
Los Dominicos, Santiago de Chile, Chile

Architects:
Felipe Assadi, Christophe Rousselle

Assistants:
Architecture: Jorge Manieu
Landscaping: Piera Sartori

Site area:
1000 m²

Gross built area:
370 m²

End of construction:
2006-03-21

Photographs:
Contributed by Felipe Assadi

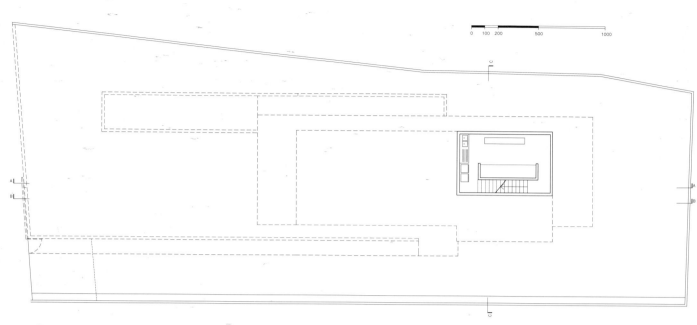

Basement plan

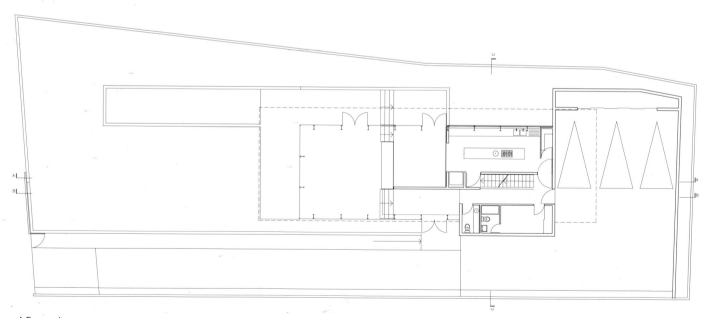

Ground floor plan

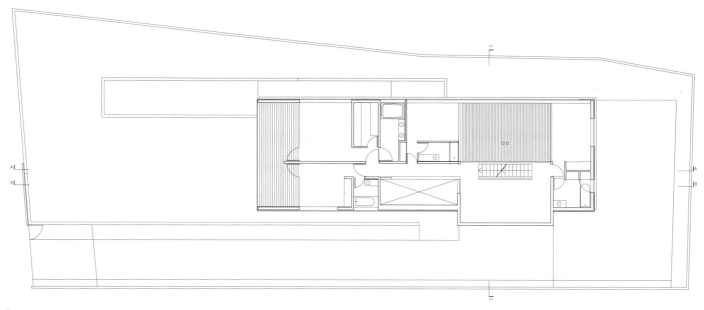

First floor plan

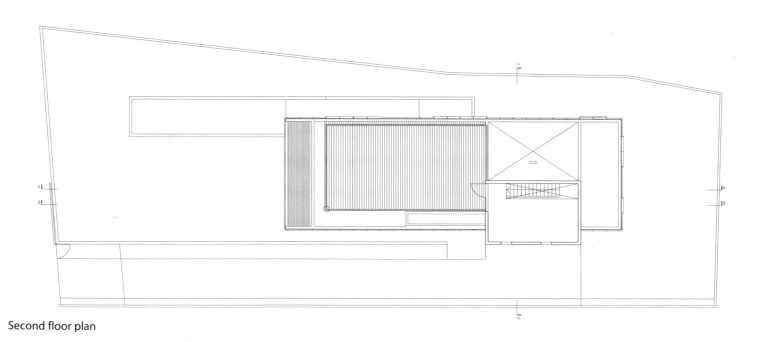

Second floor plan

111

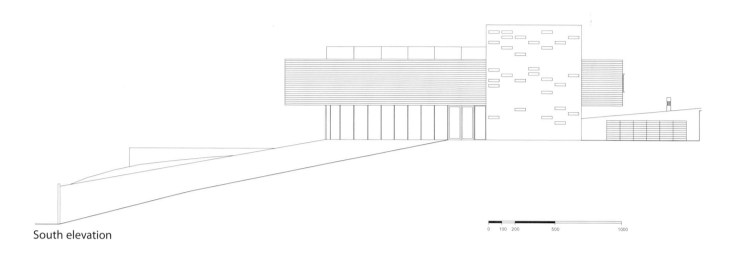

South elevation

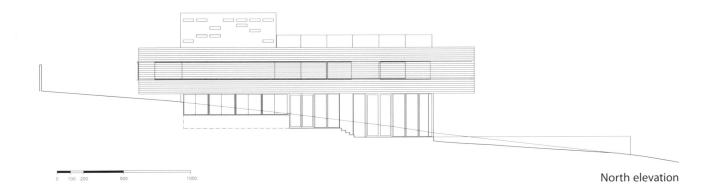

0 100 200   500   1000

Section AA

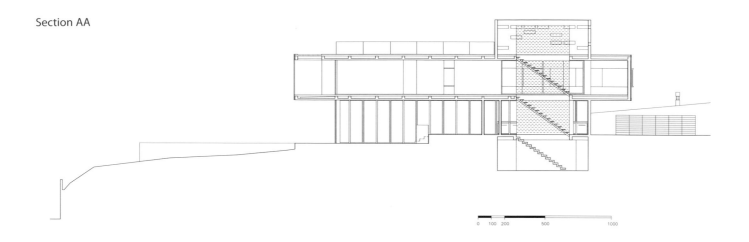

| 0 | 100 | 200 | | 500 | | 1000 |

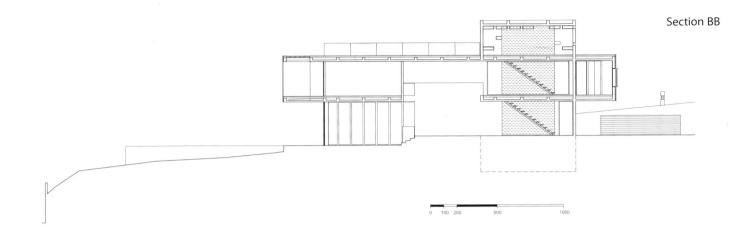

Section BB

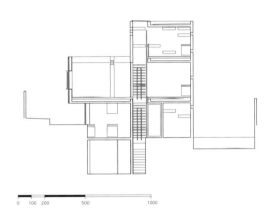

Section CC

115

Peter Ebner + Franziska Ullmann

House O. + H.

With its sloping lines in unexpected places and numerous voids cut from the structure seemingly at random, this house near Salzburg is as much an exercise in sculpture as it is in architecture.

However, while the overall look may give a first impression of being haphazard, in reality, every detail has been carefully thought out. Where a void seems to serve no purpose, closer inspection reveals perfectly-framed views of the foothills of the Alps. The sensation of these windows being mere openings rather than proper windows is heightened by their lying flush with the walls, sometimes on the inner face, sometimes on the outer.

The combination window/skylight in the master bedroom appears from the outside to have been removed from the structure as an afterthought. From the inside, its unusual placement makes it a guaranteed source of natural light whatever the time of day or season.

Contrary to first impressions, the layout is a logical progression of rooms. The main linear tract houses the entrance and bedrooms. Adjoining this is an L-shaped section containing the daily living areas, which are set half a story lower. In places, the continuous pale maple flooring, consisting of strips of different widths, folds and continues upward to form the wall cladding.

In keeping with its unconventional form, the exterior has been painted a deep red, enhancing the contrast between this house and the neighboring constructions. Depending on the lighting conditions, the house shimmers alternately in bronze and reddish tones; this is due to the transparent coat of paint containing metal particles that was applied over the terracotta-colored undercoat of the rendered brick walls.

The home's conceptual distance is accentuated by screening off most of the house from outside views, providing a sense of privacy. An enclosed private courtyard sits next to the ground floor sauna and is just as much a part of the layout as the interior spaces.

Location:
Salzburg- Bergheim, Austria
Architects:
Peter Ebner + Franziska Ullmann
Principal Designteam:
Peter Ebner
Project team:
Silvia Lechner, Florian Zimmermann, Sebastian Mävers
Client:
Doris + Stefan O.
Design:
2001
Construction:
2002-2003
Site:
935 m²
Surface - upperground:
225 m²
Surface - underground:
110 m²
Cost:
435.000 €
Photographs:
Margherita Spiluttini, Vienna

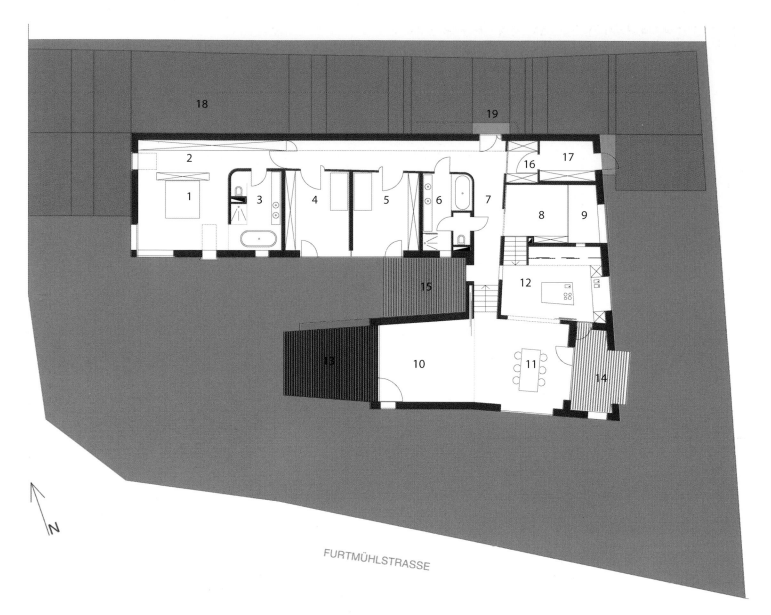

FURTMÜHLSTRASSE

N

Ground floor plan

1. Master bedroom

2. Wardrobe

3. Bathroom – parents

4. Children's Bedroom

5. Children's Bedroom

6. Bathroom – Children

7. Corridor

8. Office

9. Patio

10. Living room

11. Dining room

12. Kitchen

13. Terrace

14. Morning terrace

15. Intimate terrace

16. Cloakroom

17. Storage

18. Driveway

19. Entrance

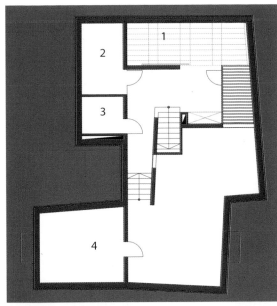

Basement plan

1. Sauna
2. Laundry
3. Mechanical room
4. Storage

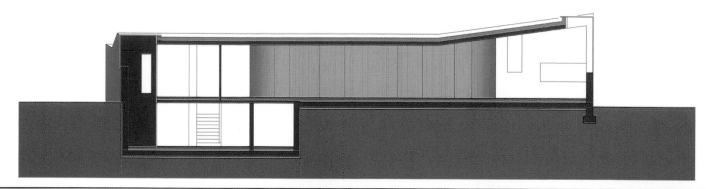

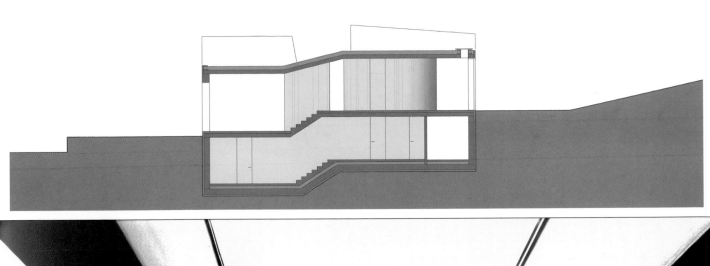

123

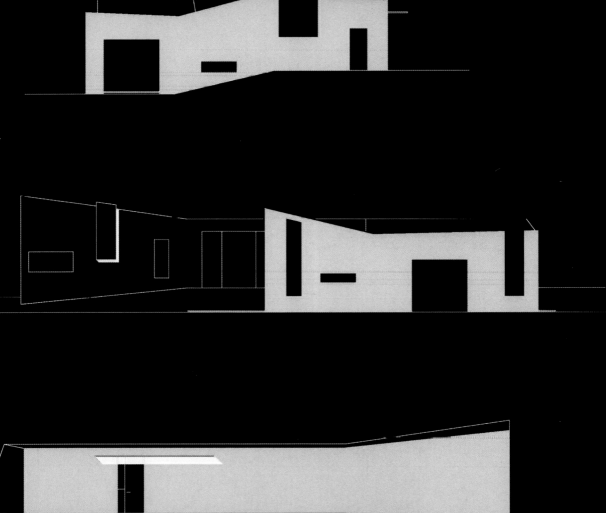

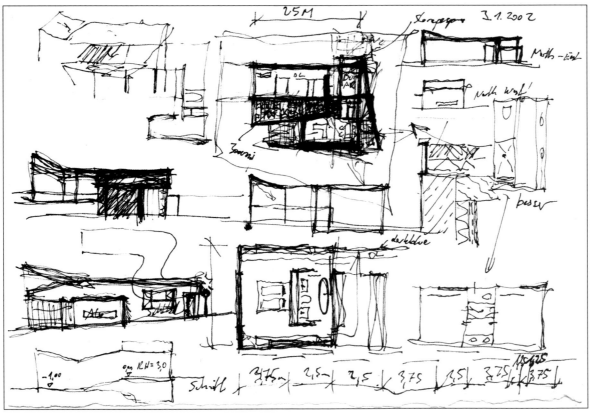

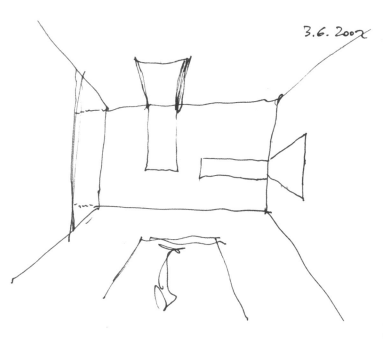

3.6. 2002

Dawson Brown Architecture

Bungan Beach House

Located on a steep 50°, southeast-facing slope high above Bungan Beach to the north of Sydney, the site is partially surrounded by natural heath land. It enjoys spectacular views of the beach and flanking rocky headlands, as well as of the northern coastline.

The program brief called for a permanent home for a working couple that would have separate functions for accommodating guests, living and working. The inspiration for the design were the simple mono-pitched fibro beach shacks of the 1950s and 60s translated into a modern architectural vernacular.

The house consists of a series of timber pavilions arranged around a sun-drenched courtyard. The site has been extensively terraced with stone retaining walls; zig-zag stairs wind up and between the pavilions.

The pavilions enable a southeast orientation and spacious outdoor decks, while at the same time separating work, sleep and living functions. Their small-size, furthermore, keeps the house as a whole from visually dominating the stunning natural surroundings. Their presence as structures in the landscape is further diminished by the use of dark-toned materials.

The large overhangs and high stone walls shield the glazed spaces from the neighboring buildings while providing protection from the summer sun and rain.

Terraced into the hillside, the building is set on a high stone base, an extension of the massive existing stone retaining wall adjoining the driveway. These stone walls crisscross the site, stabilizing the hill and providing level ground on which to build. The pavilions sit above the walls, deliberately creating the dramatic effect of houses perched on a cliff.

The buildings are of steel clad in timber with metal roofs. Floors are of blackbutt stone and walls are lined in hoop pine plywood. Outside, the decks are of teak and copper hoods protect windows and doors from the notorious rain and wind of the area's storm season.

The building relies on the ever-present sea breezes in the summer for natural cooling and also consumes minimal energy for heating in the winter due to its orientation and use of fireplaces.

Priniciple Architect:
Rob Brown
Project Architect:
Aaron Cook
Engineer:
Murtagh Bond – Ken Murtagh
Builder:
Thiessen Projects, Daniel Thiessen
Location:
Bungan Beach, Sydney, Australia
Photographs:
Richard Powers

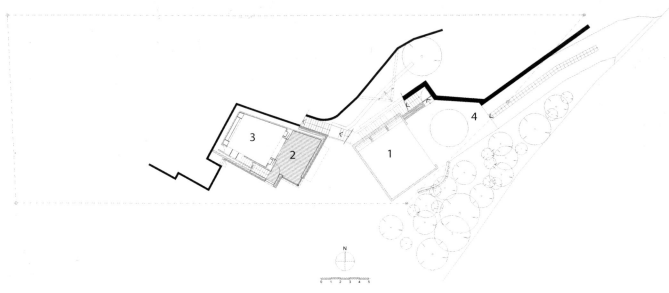

Lower level plan

1. Garage
2. Gym
3. Theatre
4. Driveway

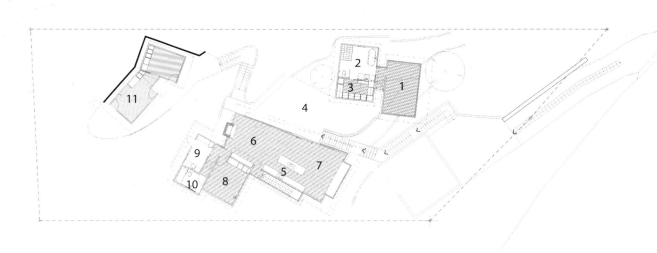

Upper level plan

1. Bedroom 1
2. Ensuite
3. Wardrobe
4. External deck
5. Kitchen
6. Living area

7. Dining area
8. Bedroom 2
9. Laundry
10. Bathroom
11. Office/Studio

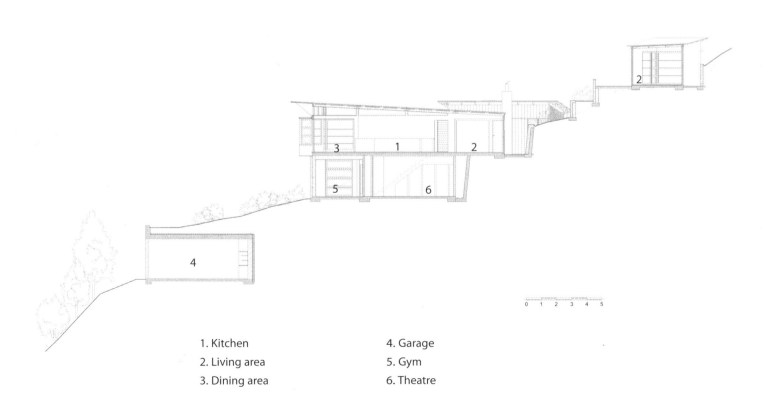

1. Kitchen

2. Living area

3. Dining area

4. Garage

5. Gym

6. Theatre

Caramel Architekten & Friedrich Stiper

House_H

After a successful collaboration in 2000, the clients commissioned this same architectural team and interior designer to design their private residence, which required space for two adults and three children.

The site that the architects chose for the house was a southeast-facing plot on the slope of the Pöstlingberg hill sitting north of the center of the city of Linz. The price was steep, but the breathtaking views of the city and the Alps more than justified the choice. It did mean, however, that the site, measuring 820 square meters in area, had to be used as efficiently as possible.

The shape of the lot was the decisive parameter for how the building was eventually placed on the lot, with three of its four sides set on the limits of the site's buildable area. Underground, the building reaches even further, to the border between private and public property (i.e., the street).

The vertical stacking of functions within the house was another way of maximizing the outdoor space: there are only 46 square meters of remaining outdoor space that cannot be used. Most of the roof of the ground floor is covered by a larch wood deck, forming a spacious terrace with ample views in all directions. The cantilevered second floor body extends a full 13.5 meters over the children's playground, thereby providing a shield from too much sun and shelter from the rain.

The ground floor is embedded cozily into the slope of the hill on one side, opening toward the yard on the other. This floor contains the master bedroom, two bathrooms and three bedrooms for the children. A fitness room, workshop and wine cellar complete the functions of this volume.

The middle level forms a connecting nucleus between the hermetic, firmly rooted ground floor and the gravity-defying, glazed top floor. The top two floors are bent at a 135° angle in relation to the lower floor, creating space for the large roof terrace over the bedrooms.

A living rooms sits half a level up from the middle floor, while an entertaining/lounge area occupies the dramatic, light-filled uppermost volume. The floor to ceiling glazing is accentuated on its top and bottom edges by a slender strip (15 cm) of steel over reinforced concrete.

Polyurethane foil, sprayed onto a layer of orientated strand board (OSB), was used to provide a homogenous cladding on the ceiling and walls. The façade facing the yard can be completely closed off by a curtain wall with stable units and sliding doors made from high pressure laminate (HPL) boards.

Location:
Linz, Austria

Architects:
Caramel Architekten ZT - Gmbh
Günter Katherl, Martin Haller,
Ulrich Aspetsberger

Interior design:
Atelier Tummelplatz -
Friedrich Stiper

Team:
Clemens Kirsch, Barbar aSchwab,
Ulrich Aspetsberger, Günter Katherl

Structural design and construction:
Werkraum Wien Zt Gmbh

Garden design:
Doris Pühringer

Planning phase :
07/2002-04/2003

Completion:
03/2004

Photographs:
Hertha Hurnaus

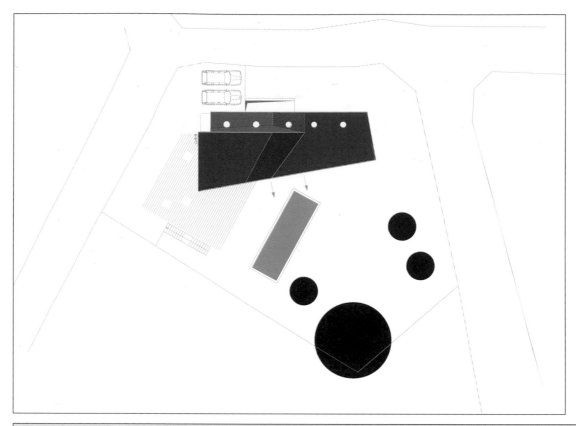

Ground floor plan

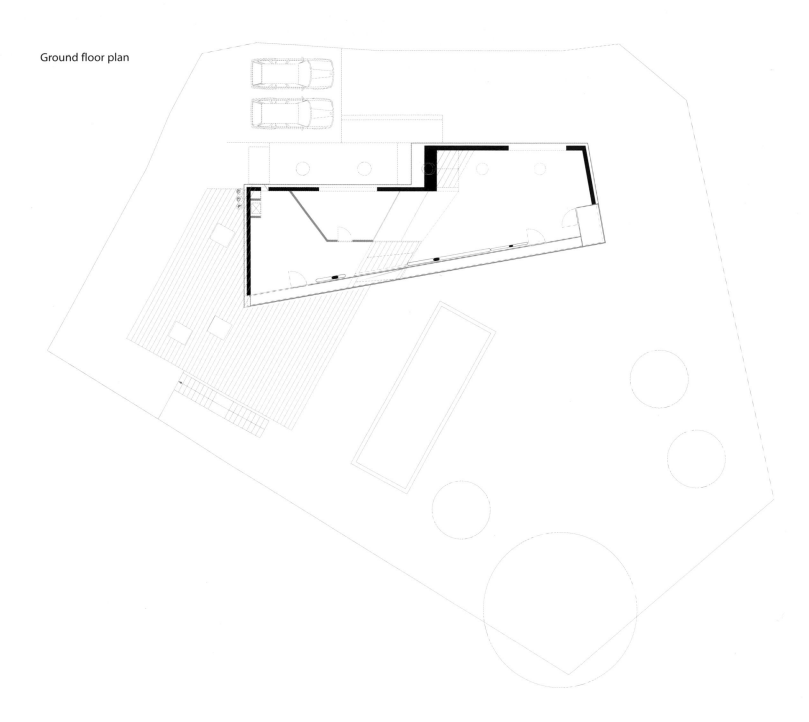

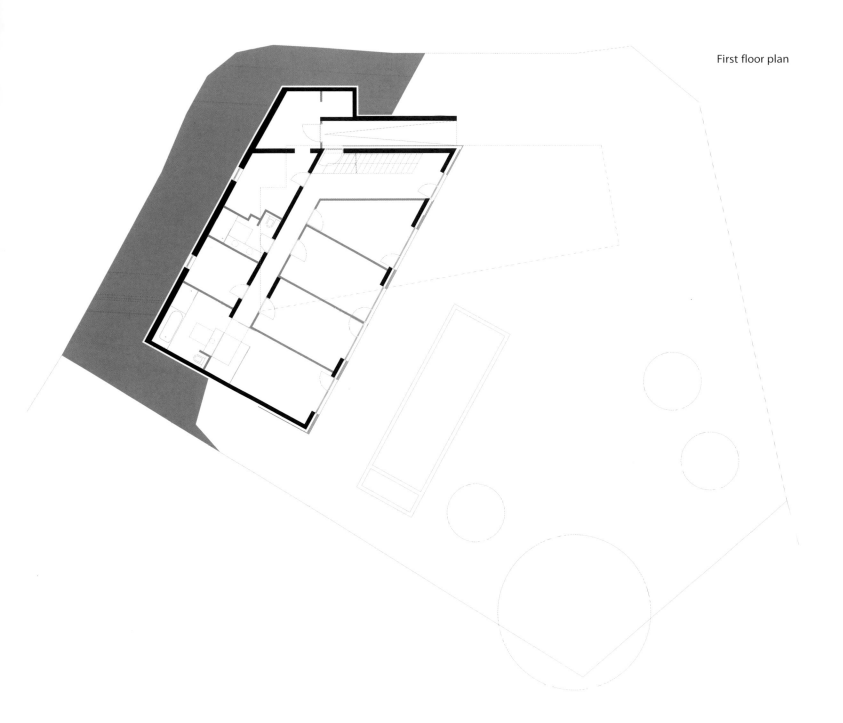

First floor plan

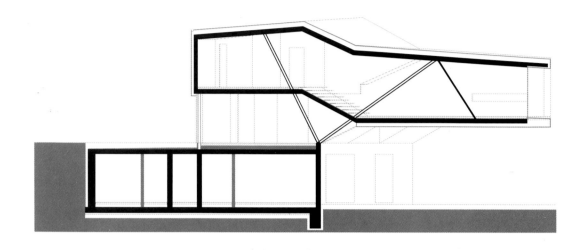

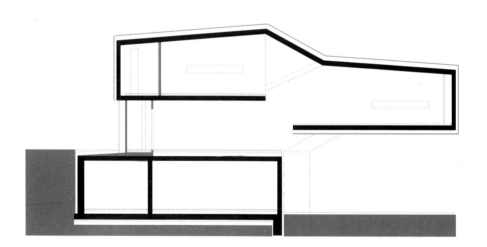

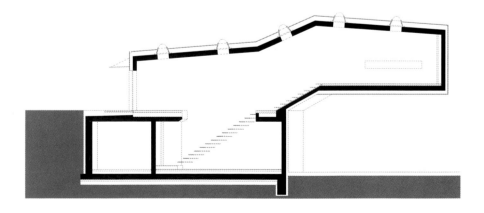

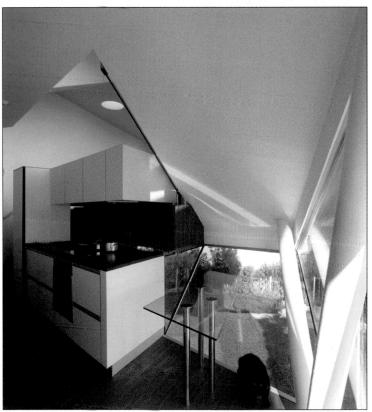

Noriyuki Tajima + tele-design

C2House

The house is on a hill 20 minutes from central Tokyo, at the end of a street in a densely populated residential area. The house accommodates a couple and an elder relative. Maximum use of natural light as a priority generated the concept stacking up three cubes. The surrounding context is tightly packed with two or three-floor houses. It is almost impossible to get direct southern sun-light or suficient garden space. The size of the lots ranges between 50 and 70 m2 and the buildings cover about 60 % of the available site area.

The south side is completely blocked by a three storey building; light and ventilation must be carefully monitored by taking advantage of available space along the narrow street to the west and the air-space above the eastern neighbor's access path. This reaffirmed the idea of the three-cube stack, to make the best of the urban context of the area.

The inside space is vertically elastic; the north and east façades read as a single unit due to the space they share and the terrace on each floor. The three volumes in the stack are comfortably connected by flights of stairs and each floor has openings facing different directions around the cubic volume. Thus, as one rises from level to level, a sequence of changes appears. The first floor faces the private garden to the east, the second floor living room and dining area receive a feeling of amplitude through the upper side-windows; on the third floor you feel like floating out through the open window. A wide flight of stairs rises up the northern side of the top cube, connecting the second floor to the roof terrace. The roof-terrace overlooks the whole area beyond the neighboring rooftops. A dynamic uplifting is experienced, as each successive roof terrace creates a territory of diffuse privacy. For the inhabitants of Tokyo a roof terrace is perceived as a symbol of unconstrained elasticity.

Location:
Shinagawa, Tokyo, Japan
Architects:
Noriyuki Tajima + tele-design
Floor Area:
115 m2
Structure:
Wood
Completion date:
June 2003
Photographs:
Kozo Takayama

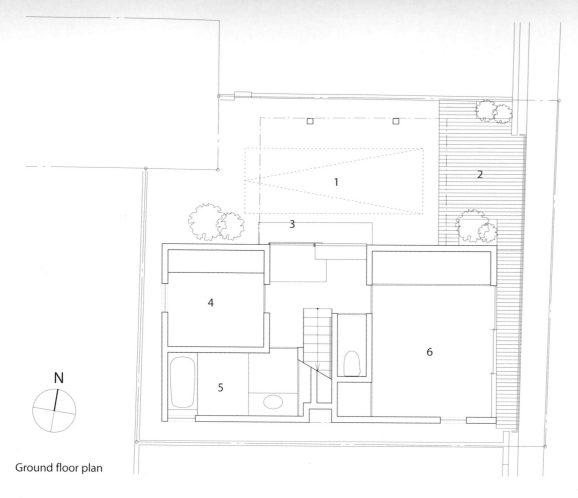

Ground floor plan

N

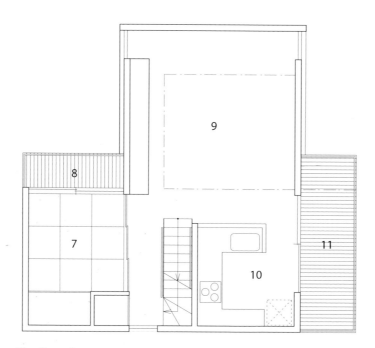

First floor plan

1. Parking
2. Terrace 1
3. Entrance
4. Packing space
5. Bathroom
6. Mother's room
7. Japanese room
8. Terrace 2
9. Living & dining room
10. Kitchen
11. Terrace 3
12. Spare room
13. Bed room
14. Terrace 4
15. Roof terrace

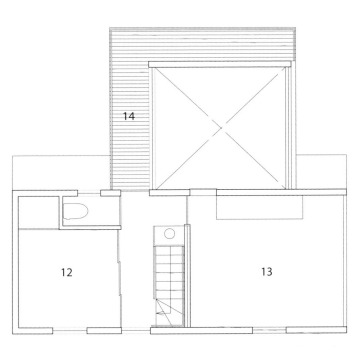

14

12

13

Second floor plan

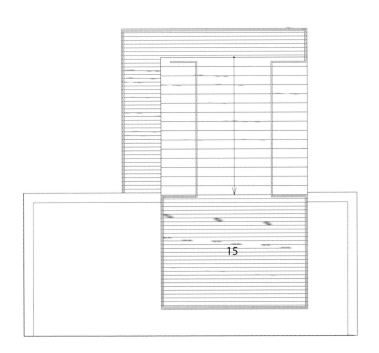

15

Third floor plan

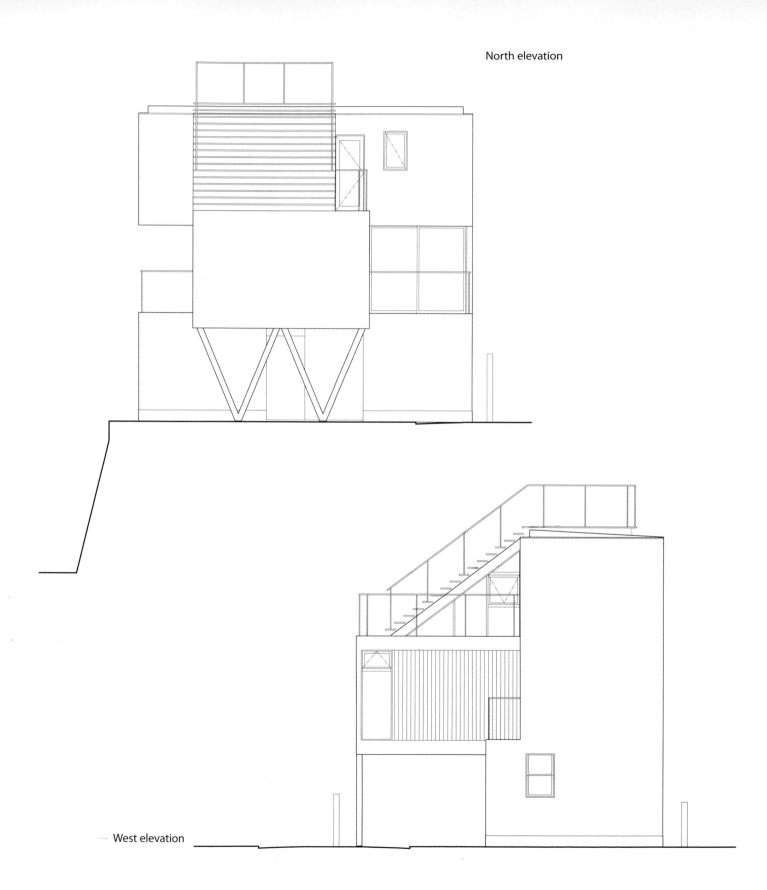

North elevation

West elevation

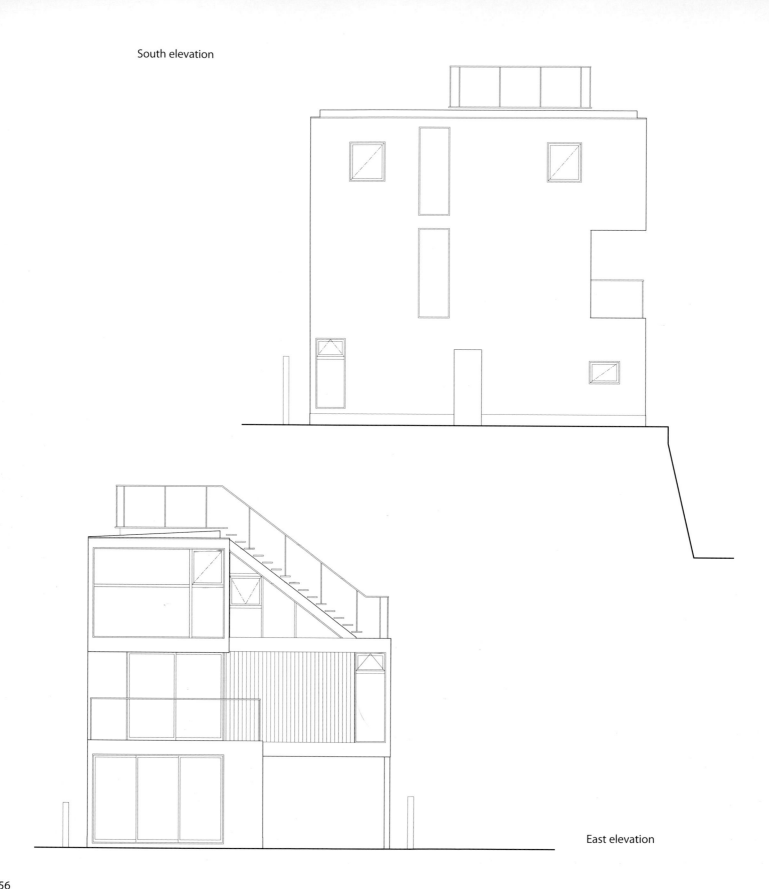

South elevation

East elevation

Stuart Tanner Architects

Pirates Bay House

This small coastal retreat near Eaglehawk Neck on Tasmania's Tasman Peninsula is a designed primarily for intermittent use. The client requested a contemporary, steel framed building that made best use of an awkward site and its coastal location. The driveway was an existing site condition that fulfilled the clients wish to park under the building.

The building is an architectural "bridge" between the landscape and sea, resting on a singular support wall that expresses that edge. A gentler dialogue with the rear of the site tempers the building's dramatic gesture toward the ocean.

The client wished to retain the principle of a coastal "shack", visually and thermally connected to the environment. The glass panels were intentionally specified as clear single skin, ensuring maximum connection and low cost. Despite this, the building performs thermally very well. Insulation in the floor, ceiling and walls, coupled with louver systems and exterior sunscreens help to keep interior temperatures ambient. Little supplementary heating is required.

All services enter the building via conduits in the main support wall. A self-contained sewage & grey water system processes waste on site. Fresh water is collected from the roof and circulated by a pump. Water is heated by gas. A cost efficient radiant ceiling system provides supplementary heating, combined with a gas water heating system ideal for an intermittently used dwelling.

The following measures increase the building's sustainability: Minimum site footprint, careful preservation of the vegetation, eradicating non-native plants and regenerating endemic species.

The simple plan has two equally sized bedrooms on the "quiet" southern edge of the building. Wet areas are all in one zone. The kitchen is a place of entertainment as well work. Decks around three sides enhance the feeling of a "floating platform for living".

The prefabricated steel frame rests on a core filled block wall. The main platform is connected to the site at the rear, suspended midway by two steel straps. Thin steel rods to footings stiffen the entire structure beneath.

Materials include blackwood exterior cladding, ship lapped, with countersunk screws plugged with Myrtle. Significant pieces of joinery are solid blackwood. The louvers are cedar.

Location:
Eaglehawk Neck, Tasmania
Architects:
Stuart Tanner Architects
Structural engineer:
Jim Gandy (Gandy Roberts Pty Ltd)
Design, documentation and approval process:
18-20 months
Construction period:
10 months
Photographs:
Brett Boardman

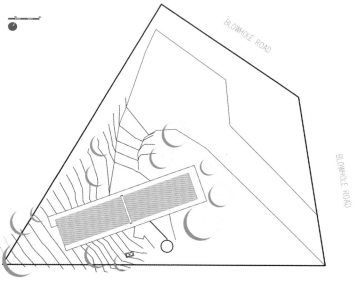

BLOWHOLE ROAD

BLOWHOLE ROAD

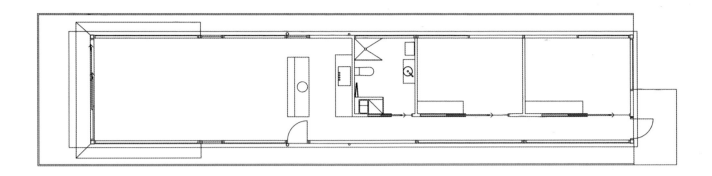

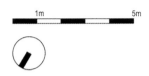

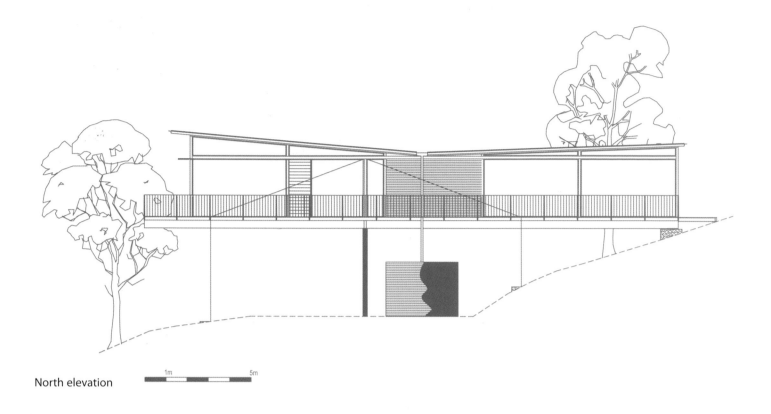

North elevation

1m   5m

Tommie Wilhelmsen

Villa Hellearmen

This 260 square meter single-family house located at Hafrsfjord on Norway's southeast coast is the result of the will to break away from the predictable sameness of standardized Scandinavian suburbia. The desire to create something playful, new and different was viewed as a value in and of itself.

The most important space in the house is, in reality, the garden. The maximum degree of fluidity between interior and exterior was sought in the design, as seen, for example, in the massive glazed surfaces that simply slide away to create nearly seamless connections. The idea was to not only bring as much of the Scandinavian seasons and light into the house, but also to take the house outward, into the garden.

The house is a highly complex structure both in plan and section, and was designed to create a number of distinct zones, all of which would be in visual and physical contact with each other. The rooms create a kind of inner topography, with an abundance of daylight flowing through. The skillfully executed contraposition of curved and straight lines provides a highly organic, fluid aspect, both inside and out, thereby achieving the desired goal of breaking the architectural mold.

Location:
Hafrsfjord, Norway
Architect:
Tommie Wilhelmsen
Lighting Design:
Fredrik Eng
Promoter:
Husgalleriet AS
Photographs:
Emile Ashley, Ashley Studio (EA)
Tommie Wilhelmsen (TW)

EA

Ground floor plan

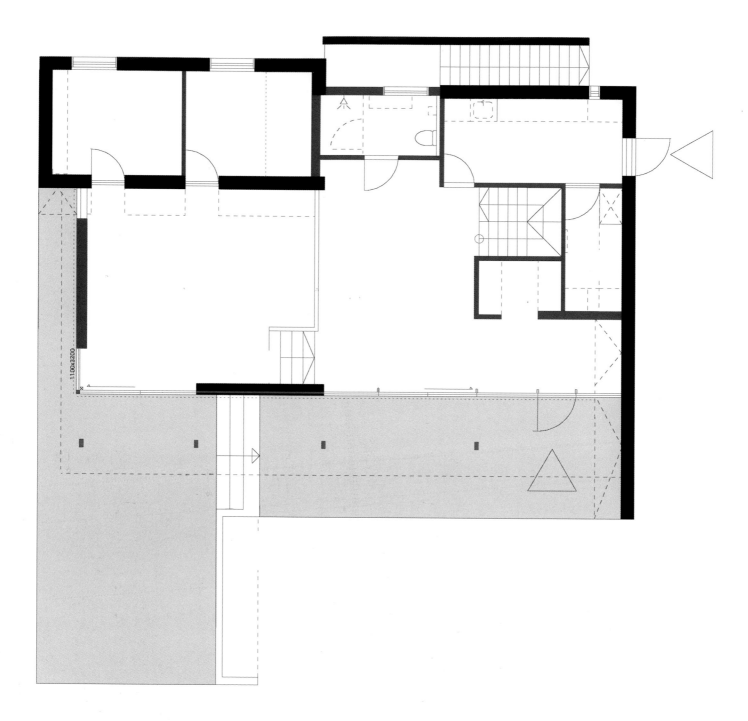

First floor plan

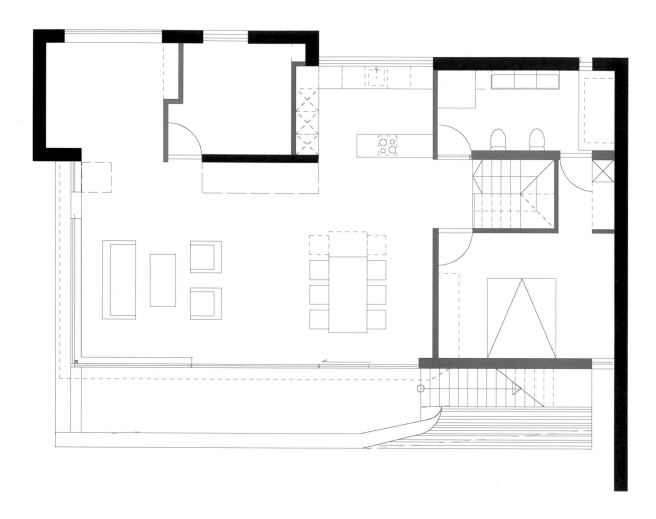

TW

TW

E. Cobb Architects

Kogan Residence

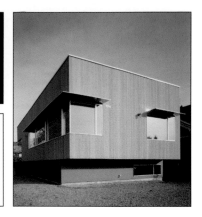

Having been described as "a tour de force of material use, detailing and extremely fluid spatial qualities", the Kogan Residence is a logical considered response to the challenge of creating a retirement home for a couple in Seattle, Washington with elements reminiscent of their native Rio de Janeiro.

The Kogans had purchased a small cottage and were against the idea of a straight renovation, preferring instead to imbue their retirement home with their own sensibilities and lifestyles. Their contractor subsequently referred the couple to the architect Eric Cobb.

Cobb, in turn, felt that with a few minor interventions, this modestly-scaled project could undergo a tremendous change. In connection with the design and construction concepts, he says "We prefer to work with non-precious, readily available materials. They allow details, proportion, light and space to characterize the work. At the same time we believe that when we are successful, these materials transcend their common associations. The assemblies are absolutely critical to the work – they are closely tied to the structural logic and presence, as well as controlled detailing."

Utilizing the existing foundation coupled with a newly integrated scheme, Cobb designed an understated 944-square-foot home that makes full use of the existing conditions regarding placement, space and light. The project's most characteristic aspect is the cantilevered façade, which adds a critical 75 square feet (6.97 sq. m.) to the single-story open floor plan.

Another is a large north facing window unit that obviates the need for extreme weather protection yet at the same time allows ample light. While the cantilever creates a desirable separation between public and private space, the raised backyard and single entryway connect the house to the surrounding landscape. Among the Kogans' favorite elements is the perimeter of Leyland Cypress saplings, which will grow to create an outdoor room off the back deck.

Location:
Seattle, WA, USA
Architect:
E. Cobb Architects
Photographs:
Steve Keating

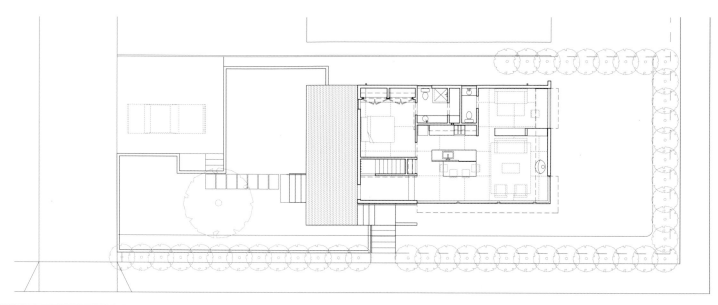

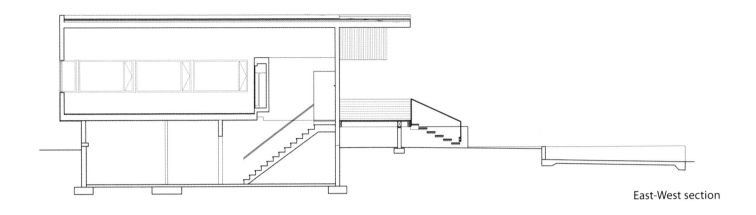

East-West section

185

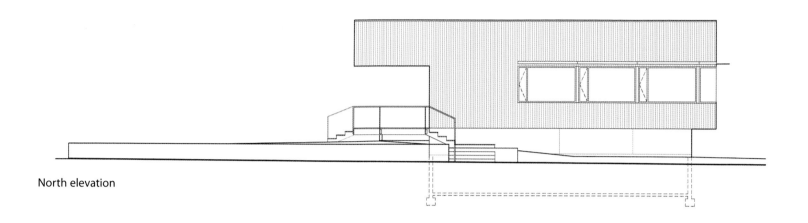

North elevation

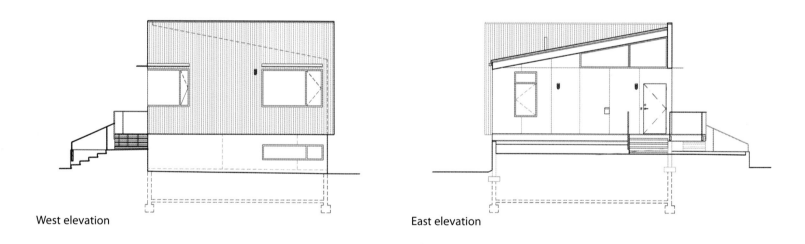

West elevation

East elevation

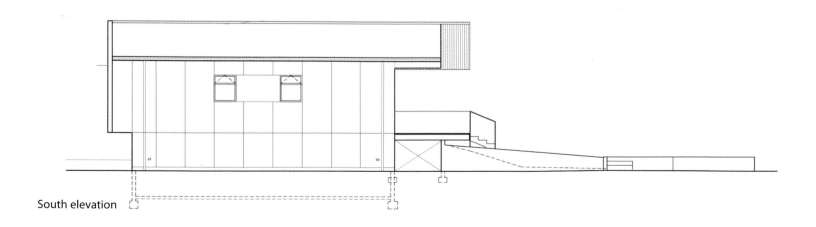

South elevation

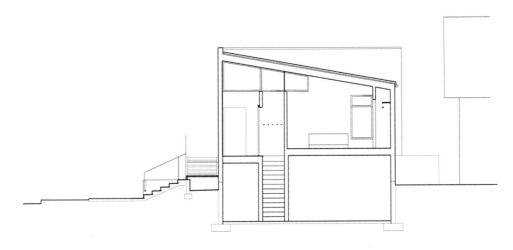

North-South section

Waro Kishi + K.ASSOCIATES/Architects

House in Higashi-Otsu

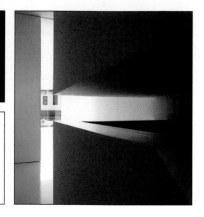

This is a residence designed for two generations of a single family, and consists of several private rooms and a living/dining space for all to gather. Nevertheless, the interior was entirely designed with white, featureless spaces that would be indifferent to their individual purposes, in an attempt to design the 'distance' that the residents would feel within this interior space.

The fact that everything inside the building is white is an important factor in creating this sense of distance. Moreover, six changes in level and a total of nearly 82 feet (25 meters) of corridors and stairs arranged within the three-story wooden structure were intended to make the inhabitants aware of the 'distance'. In contrast, the central living/dining area was planned as a large integrated space opened outward.

The challenge here involved considering interior spaces as exterior, by adopting a finish that would give the impression of an architectural interior to the very end; that is, by creating a white promenade-like space bearing a vague resemblances to some exterior landscape. In the architect's own words: "I believe that 'interior/exterior' is the most important issue in architecture. The black, matte metal plates used on the exterior finish as opposed to the white interior embody as well as emphasizes this issue. At the same time, it illustrates my wish that this architecture should feed upon the meandering suburban landscape."

The structural system used for the house is almost exclusively timber. The total built floor area of the house is 2390 sq ft (222 m²), with a footprint of 1270 sq ft (118 m²).

Location:
Higashi-Otsu, Shiga Pref., Japan
Architect:
Waro Kishi +K.ASSOCIATES/
Architects
Design:
10/2001 - 07/2002
Construction:
08/2002 - 04/2003
Consultants:
Urban Design Institute
General contractor:
Kunisada Komuten Co.,Ltd
Structural system:
timber
Site area:
198.37 m²
Building area:
118.10 m²
Total floor area:
222.39 m²
Photographs:
Hiroyuki Hirai

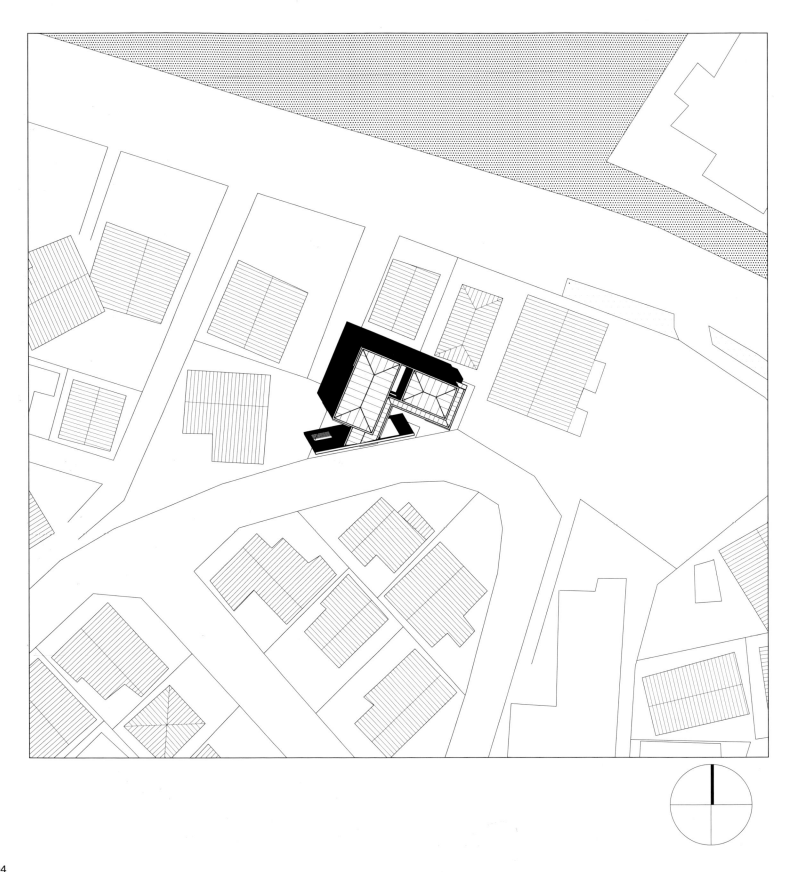

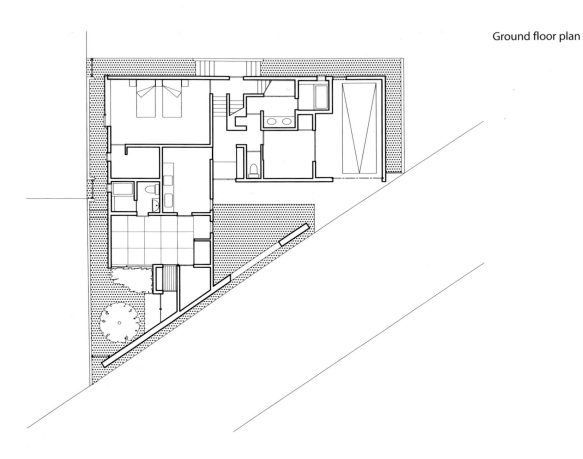

Ground floor plan

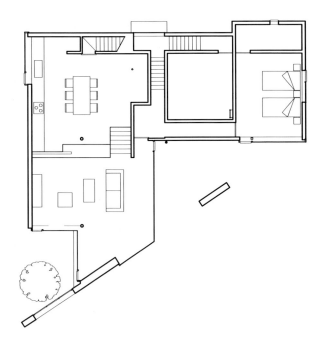

First floor plan

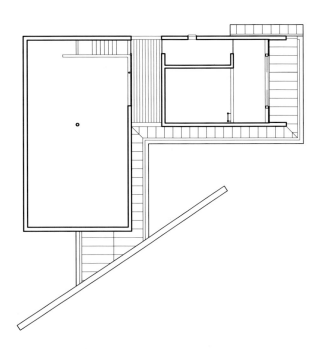

Second floor plan

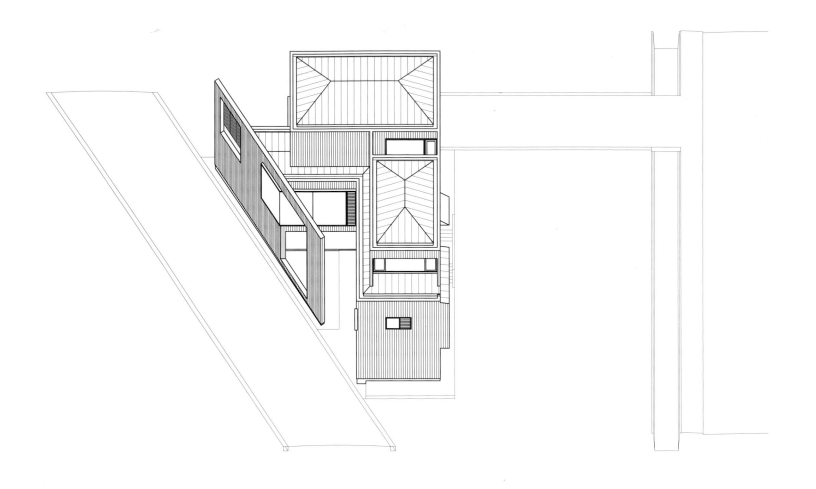

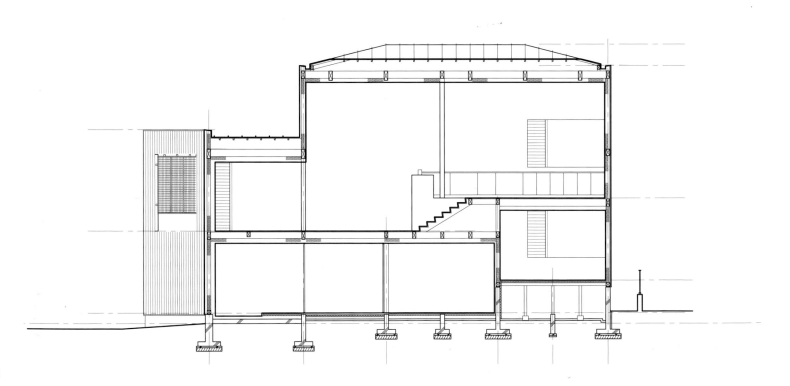

Office of Mobile Design, Jennifer Siegal

Seatrain House

This 3,000 square foot residence is situated in a 300-loft live-and-work artist community by the Brewery. Industrial and traditional materials are playfully combined, using storage containers and steel found on-site in downtown LA.

Large panels of glass throughout the house open up the space, allowing natural light to pour in, connecting it to the rest of the community. The project has been a collaborative experiment between the client and the builders, where creative and structural decisions were made as the house was being constructed.

This home literally grows up from the land around it, engaging with and incorporating the industrial history of downtown LA by using found-on-site materials. Grain trailers are transformed into a koi fishpond and a lap pool. The large storage containers are used to create and separate the dwelling spaces within the house. Each storage container has its own individual function, one is the entertainment and library area, another is a dining room and office space overlooking the garden below, another serves as the bathroom and laundry room and yet another is the master bedroom, a visually dramatic protruding volume that wraps around the upper part of the house. This unfussy space allows for the dynamic interplay of materials and forms, the contrast of corrugated metals, industrial containers and exposed wooden beams all highlighted with warm, calm green hues.

All of the containers used in the house have been altered in surprising ways. Some have been severed into separate pieces, others have been added onto, layered or wrapped, showing the myriad design possibilities in repurposing these materials. There are wrapped design elements throughout the house including a 12-foot high steel plate fence that wraps around the entire site. It lifts up at one point, stretching to become a canopy that shades the entrance, creating the feeling that the ground tilts upward. Here, recycled materials are not just practical and cost effective; they create a unique, dramatic architectural vocabulary. Combined with steel and glass, the result is sculptural, open and LA modern, creating an oasis without disguising the industrial source of inspiration.

Location:
Brewery, Los Angeles, California, USA

Design Team:
Principal: Jennifer Siegal
Senior Designer: Kelly Bair
Assistant: Andrew Todd

Creative Director & General Contractor:
Richard Carlson

Interior Design:
Arkkit Forms / David Mocarski

Landscape Design:
James Stone

Waterscape Design:
Jim thompson

Water Features:
Liquid Works / Rik Jones

Steel Fabrication:
Steel Man / Don Griggs

Glass Fabrication:
Penguin Construction / Gadie Aharoni

Artist:
Phillip Slagter

Photographs:
Undine Pröhl

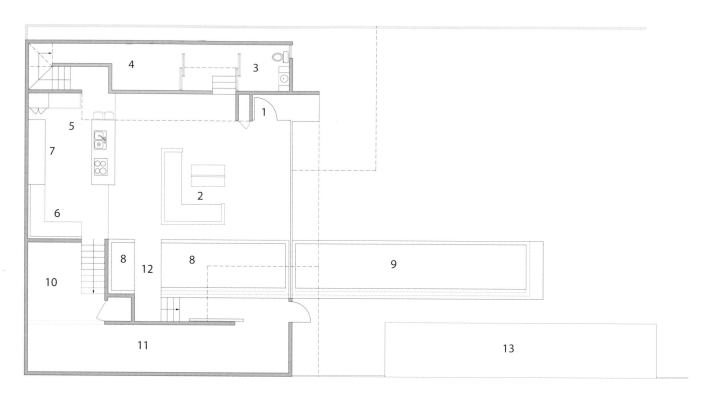

Ground floor plan

1. Entry
2. Living room
3. Guest bath
4. Utility and laundry
5. Kitchen
6. Lounge
7. Bar
8. Interior Koi pond
9. Lap pool
10. Library
11. Media room
12. Foot bridge
13. Guest house

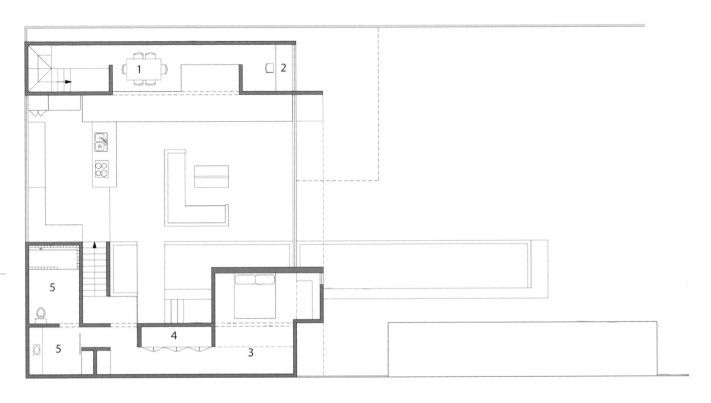

First floor plan

1. Dining room
2. Office
3. Master bedroom
4. Closet
5. Master bathroom

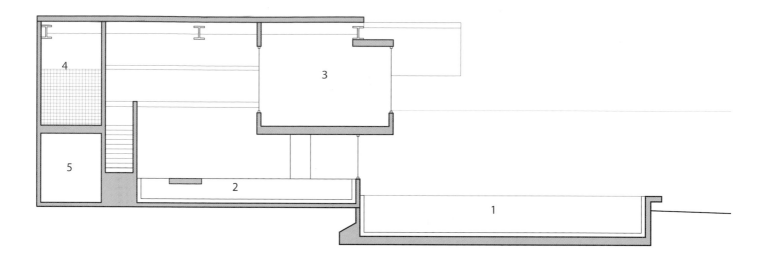

Section AA

1. Lap pool
2. Interior Koi pond
3. Master bedroom
4. Master bathroom
5. Library

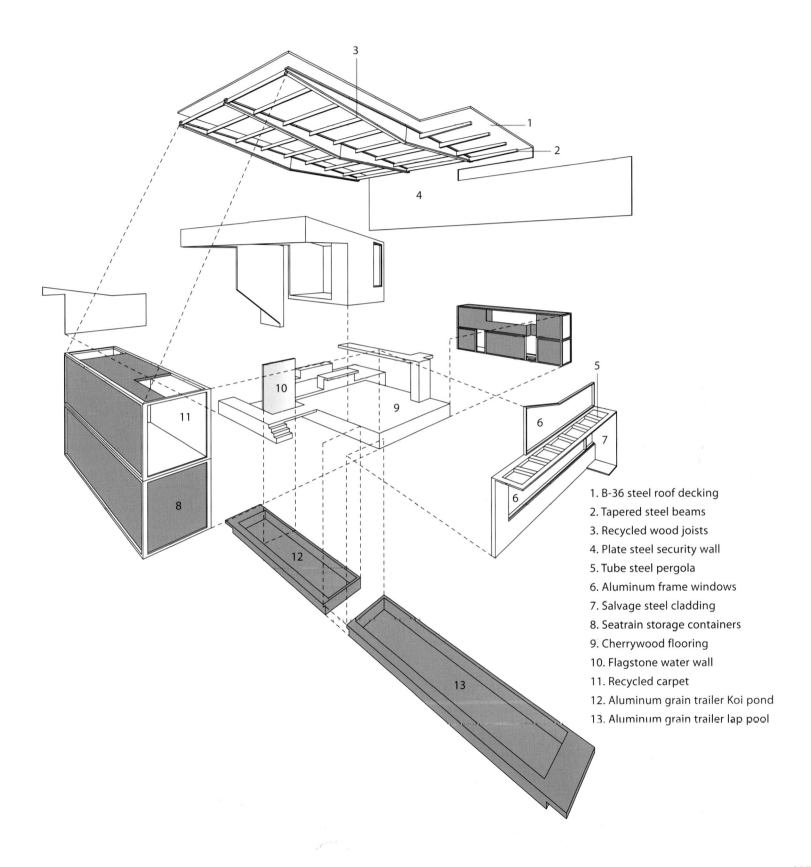

1. B-36 steel roof decking
2. Tapered steel beams
3. Recycled wood joists
4. Plate steel security wall
5. Tube steel pergola
6. Aluminum frame windows
7. Salvage steel cladding
8. Seatrain storage containers
9. Cherrywood flooring
10. Flagstone water wall
11. Recycled carpet
12. Aluminum grain trailer Koi pond
13. Aluminum grain trailer lap pool

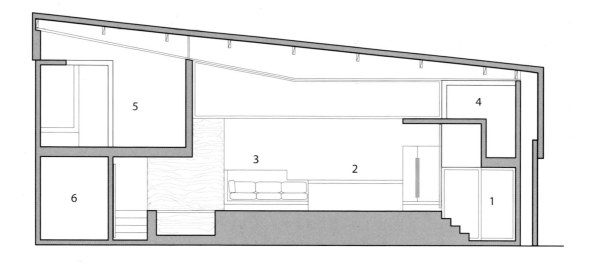

Section BB

1. Utility room   4. Dining
2. Kitchen / bar   5. Master bedroom
3. Lounge   6. Media room

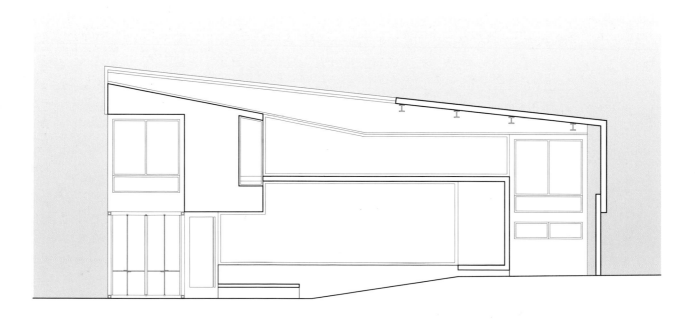

213

Jun Igarashi Architect

Kaze no wa - Wind Circle

The site is an abandoned farm surrounded by untouched woodland and fields. There is still a cow shed and a storehouse on the land. Very different from "Rectangular Forest", the architect's previous work, the program of Kaze no wa called for a place where a ceramic artist and his foster children could live together.

What the two programs had in common was the need to construct a building that was as large as the budget would allow, to house the maximum number of creative activities under one roof, without them interfering with each other, yet maintaining an interconnected spatial relation. Rather than a series of self-contained spaces leading off a long corridor, the corridor widens and becomes the space itself. Thus, the building consists of an elongated strip in the landscape, reflecting the characteristic horizontality that prevails in this unspoiled natural environment.

The exterior walls are clad with wooden ship-lapped siding. The roof has an extended overhang, to shed stormwater away from the outer walls of the house.

A number of openings are arranged rhythmically along the façade, imposing a dynamic composition upon this potentially sullen and mysterious looking building, which reflects the functional look of existing vernacular structures.

Daylight enters through the windows, orchestrating areas of more or less light throughout the day.

A dip in the grade of the terrain allows two levels to be contained at one end of the building, without altering the strict horizontal line of the house. The main floor at the opposite end splits into an upper and lower level, reached by stepped ramps. The two level area is subdivided again, to accommodate specific functions or spaces of greater privacy.

The structural frames use assemblies made into I-shaped beams using local timber, selected for use after its cost and strength had been evaluated.

The width of the building was decided at 4.55 meters, the maximum the beams would span. The ceiling height was kept low, but the length of the building extends to 43.68 meters.

Box-like volumes containing specific functions and systems interrupt the floor. Installed in a half-basement level, they seem to emerge into the huge single room, adding visual complexity. Ramps lead up and down, resulting in an enormous flowing atmosphere.

Location:
Tokoro-tyou, Tokoro-gun, Hokkaido, Japan

Architect:
Jun Igarashi Architect

Photographs:
Daichi Ano

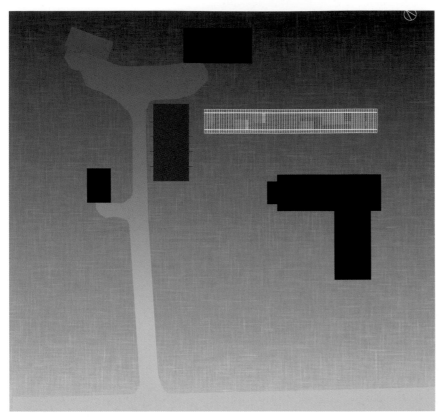

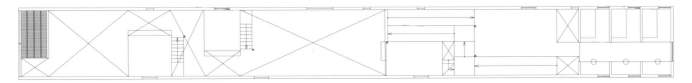

First floor plan

Ground floor plan

N 0 1 3 6m

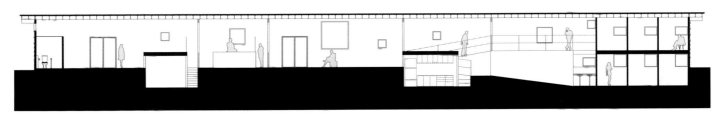

Longitudinal section

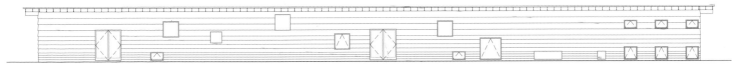

South elevation

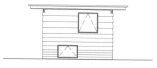

East elevation

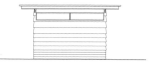

West elevation

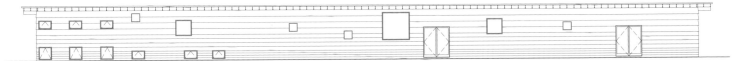

North elevation

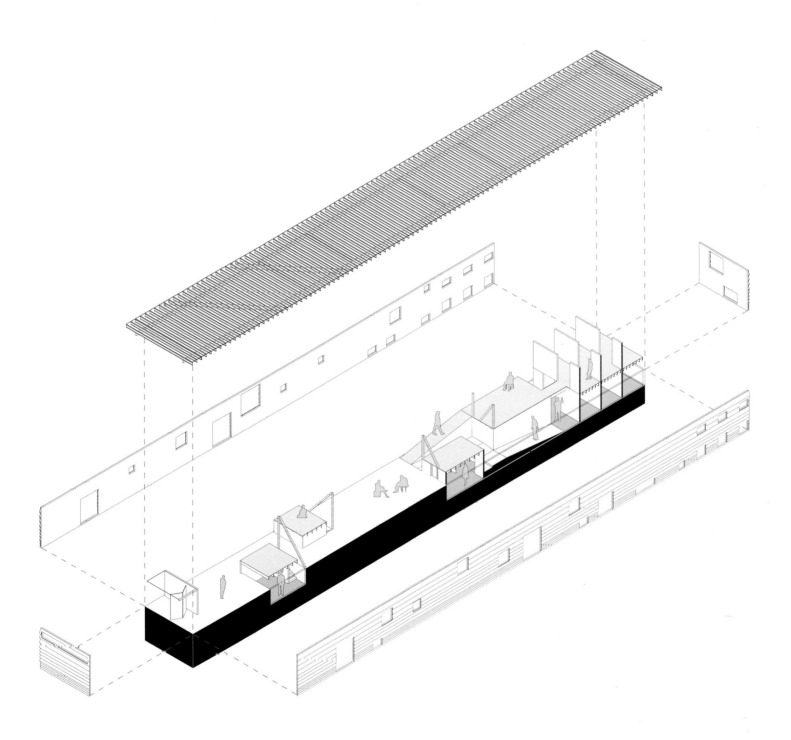

Cloud 9

Villa Bio

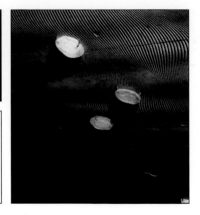

Villa Bio is the name given to this home located in the suburbs of Llers in the Spanish province of Gerona. The architect Enric Ruiz-Geli defines this as a "bio" structure as the reflection of a contemporary construction style that should serve as a platform for today's art and culture. For the architect, "inhabiting" takes place on an existing platform that can become art: the art of habitation.

This platform was conceived as a linear landscape of "events" that buckles away from the terrain and forms an increasing spiral. It is a linear concrete structure with a continuous C-shaped section. The blind lengthwise facades serve as beams and create a 15-meter projection.

The definition of the exterior enclosures was based on the precept that concrete is a liquid material that solidifies to create a "liquid" topography on the façade. The program began with a 3D model of the desired topography, like a Virilian landscape in relief. The designers used CadCam, with 3-axis milling, to create a singular, personalized 3D image measuring 24x3 meters. The mold became the formwork for the north and south facades.

The platform took on its mutant, liquid form with a green roof and interior landscape of glass blocks by Emiliana Design stamped with digital rendering. The roof features a hydroponic garden that acts as insulation and includes green LED lighting that highlights the vegetation.

The interior lighting system is varied and automatically controlled with a dynamic system that changes the color and intensity according to the natural exterior light conditions.

Location: Llers, Girona, España
Architect: Enric Ruiz-Geli
Interior design: Manel Soler Caralps
Colaborators Cloud9: Frederic Guillard, Andre Brösel, Oscar Puga
Engineer: Manel Raventós
Structure: Antonio Diosdado
Instalations: Joaquim Ribes Quintana, Toni Jordà
Green roof: Jardines Burés
Landscape: Joan Madorell
Glass: Cricursa
Graphics: Laia Jutglà
Floor: Pavindus, SA
Concrete mold: Valchromat
Kitchen furniture: Samaniego
Paint: Noucolor
Lights: Iguzzini
Photographs: Lluís Ros

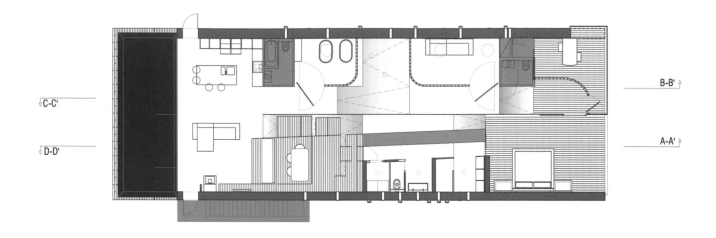

C-C'
D-D'
B-B'
A-A'

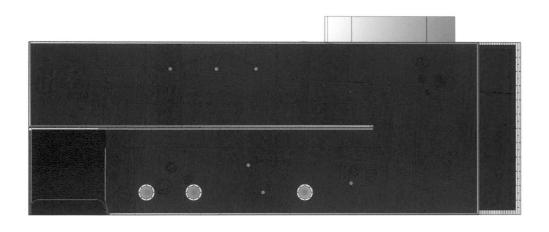

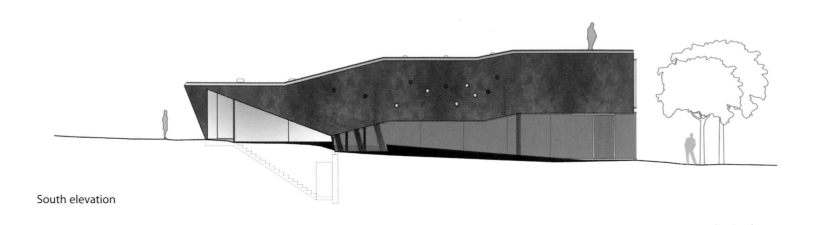

South elevation

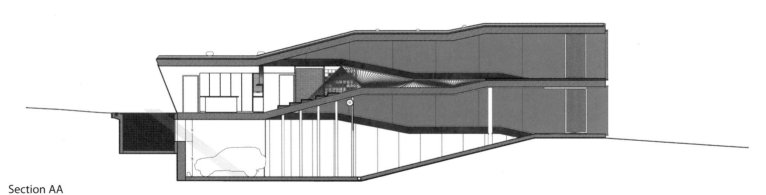

Section AA

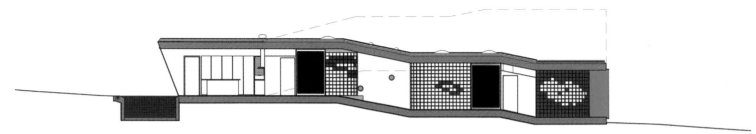

Section BB

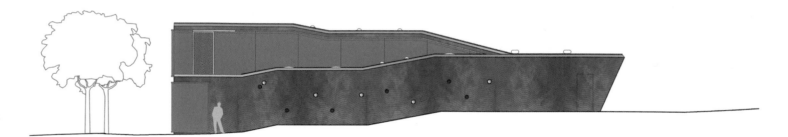

North elevation

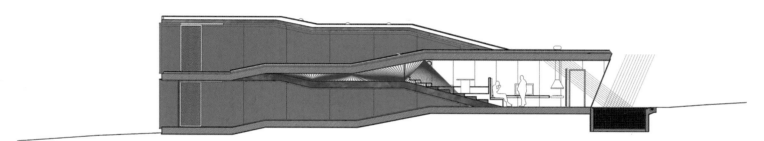

Section CC

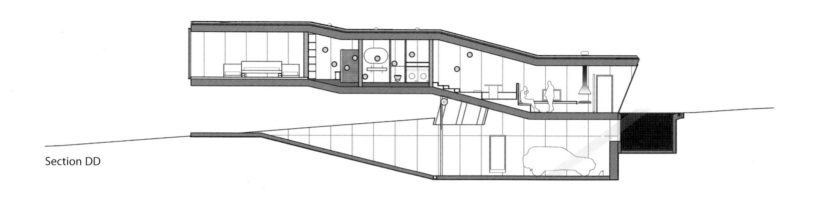

Section DD

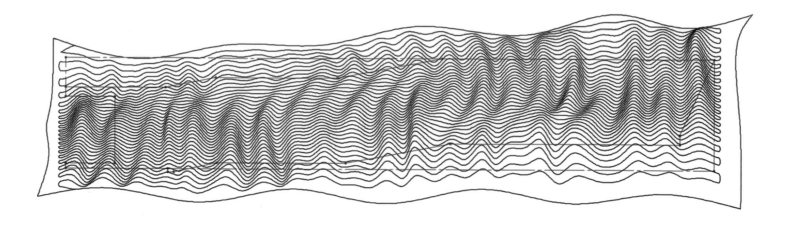

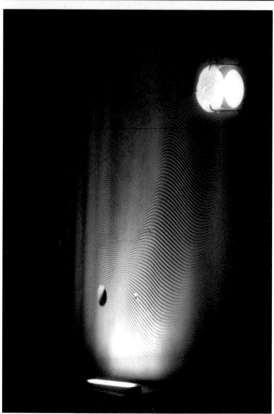

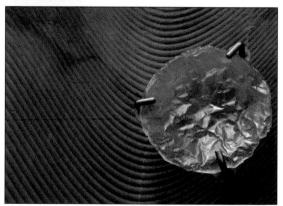

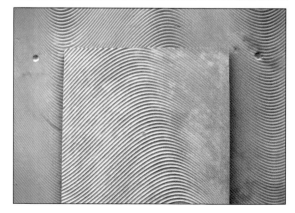